SOMETHING TELLS ME

by
Walt Cameron

"SUPERNATURAL EXPERIENCES"
Foretold by an Invisible Psychic Intelligence

DORRANCE PUBLISHING CO., INC.
PITTSBURGH, PENNSYLVANIA 15222

"SOMETHING TELLS ME"
"A TRUE STORY"

PREFACE

If the events, of which you will be reading, had occurred in the life of a famous or notable person, these stories would arouse national, if not worldwide, interest. However since they have happened to just an ordinary citizen, there may be no interest in them, other than to certain members of my family.

After some encouragement, if not outright prodding, by certain friends and family members, I have made the decision to write down numerous of these occurrences.

I do not try to explain what has happened. I merely relate it as nearly as memory permits, as accurately and concisely as possible. This is not my "Life Story" although it is necessary in order to lay the proper foundation, to tell some of my early life history. This is so that you may better know the character, or rather, cultural background of the writer.

Some of the events are just "interesting"—others are really bizarre; but they all happened in my life.

I make no apologies, I just thought others may be interested in hearing of the message to be shared with all.

INTRODUCTION

Many times during my life I have been confronted with troublesome situations or seemingly unsolvable problems; as most of us have faced at sometime.

The unusual difference seems to be that, in many of these situations I have had a sudden impulse of inspired knowledge, which has resulted in a solution to the problem.

Some of this inspired knowledge has come to me in technical solutions above and beyond any training or experience I possessed.

In some cases the *something* that tells me is just a hunch, or inspiration; in other cases it is as though something or someone is actually speaking to me, in a kind of thought language, rather than an audible voice.

Had I never met my wife or her father, I probably would never have realized, or learned of, the existence of parapsychology and would have gone on thinking I was really "smart" to have solved some of these problems.

There have been numerous incidents in my career when high-up officials have told me I was one of the smartest men they had ever met. I would just smile modestly and thank them. I would not have dared to tell them that it was not really my idea at all, that some mysterious *something* had told me how to do things.

In this book I try to relate a number of these incidents, along with some other interesting stories that are a small part of my travel through this most marvelous thing we call "life."

W. E. Cameron

We begin with a nostalgic poem, written by my older sister, Edith M. Cameron, which will set the tone for the "way it was" on the mountain-top farm in central Pennsylvania during the twenties—the years between World War I and the Great Depression of the thirties.

"Christmas Was Special"

I remember a long ago Christmas
When Mama cooked and cleaned.
She stayed up late, to make a quilt
For my doll bed yet unseen.

Daddy and my brother, Bob
Trudged through the drifted snow.
From the deep pine woods on the farm,
With a freshly hewn tree in tow.

It filled the corner of the room,
So tall it touched the ceiling.
While tenderly Daddy trimmed the tree,
We kids choked up with feeling.

The Christmas program at the church,
We viewed with raptured glee.
The horse-drawn sleigh with tinkling bells,
Made the ride seem like magic to me.

Moonlight glistened on the driven snow
For the two mile ride back home.
Our songs filled the air, our hearts rejoiced,
The most wonderful time I've known.

Tucked deep in a corner of my heart,
I carry these lovely scenes.
Each Christmas I open My secret place,
And re-live those cherished dreams.

Edith M. Cameron
Prescott Valley, Arizona
February 18, 1992

CHAPTER I
DADDY ON THE FARM

My story begins (just a few days before my actual entry into this world,) on a Friday evening when my father returned from work to the little farm in Indiana County, Pennsylvania, where it is beautiful this time of year—early May.

His concern was greater than usual about conditions at a small railroad company. He was a conductor there and sometimes rode the caboose of the long coal drags being shuttled from the mine to the main lines for shipment, and sometimes operated the "gas car," Number 99—a large streetcar-like machine that provided passenger service over the tracks of the Cambria and Indiana Railroad which ran through Cambria and Indiana Counties.

That Friday, May 6th, 1927, his mind was not on the farm chores, or the cares of his little family, his lovely wife of ten years, Edna Pearl and three children, Robert ten years, Edith nine years, and Charles four and a half years of age. That night at the supper table (In Pennsylvania farm country the evening meal is called "supper"), he was telling Edna about a serious derailment on the Railroad; all the employees had been pressed into service to help clean up the wreck.

Walter—Albert Waldo Cameron—was telling Edna that he didn't like the way one of the railroad crane cars was rigged. He had told the gang boss that it should be tied down better and that someone was gong to be killed if it fell over. His suggestion was met with a scoff, and he was told he should mind his own business. But this was a matter of such concern that he had broken his custom of never

1

bringing work home to his family. He feared that someone may be injured—or killed—during the derailment clean up.

Saturday morning came, and so did the duties of his hundred-acre farm. His mind turned to milking the family cows, and to the neighboring farmers who had come by to discuss the prospect of a few beautiful plowing and planting days ahead. They had tried to persuade Walter to lay off work for the planting. Ordinarily he would have done so, but now, with the derailment, he felt he must go to work Monday morning.

Sunday evening Edna, being very near to the delivery time of her fourth child (the writer), did not feel up to going to evening services at the Strongstown Methodist Church. The children were not always expected to attend evening service, since they had attended Sunday School and the morning service. So Walter went alone to the church.

I can only remember listening to my mother's stories of events, naturally, but one I always have had vividly emblazoned in my mind occurred that Sunday evening when Walter returned from services. With a radiant smile, he came into the small, country cottage and began to tell Edna of the glorious time he had had at the service: He even had gone forward at altar call to make a recommitment, although he and Edna both already had been "saved" and were spiritual folks, to say the least. But that night, Edna said, she saw a radiant glow like a halo about my father's head as he entered the room, a radiance that shone with all the colors of the rainbow and she knew he must have had a really glorious experience with God, for she had never before ever seen or heard of such a thing.

Monday morning was chilly, almost frosty, but promising to be another beautiful, sunny spring day. After milking Starry, the only remaining milk cow because Spotty was too ornery to milk, and so became beef, for the family larder. Walter—or, "Wally" as most folks called him—couldn't get the model T Ford started, and already he was running late, since the alarm, for some strange reason, had failed to ring that morning, so he had overslept. Now the car wouldn't start and he couldn't find his gloves, which were a must for work and would help him turn the crank to get the car started.

The men came by again to try to persuade him to stay home, since he was already going to be late for work but he would not.

He finally got the old Ford started, then shouted into the window of the little farm house, and waved the gloves, which he had now located, as a signal to Edna that he was leaving to go to work.

On the job (the derailment was not more than a mile or two from the little farm) it was now about 8:30 A.M. and Wally was walking beside the crane car he had complained about just as it was hooking up to a derailed car full of coal.

Suddenly he heard someone shout, "Jump Wally, jump! Look out!" As he stepped up his pace to run from the falling crane car, his left shoelace got hooked on one of the lacing hooks of his right high-top shoe, tripping him. He fell face down, with arms raised in a defensive motion, as he became the man whom he had worried may be killed, and the giant crane settled down on top of him. This man, who was about to become a father for the fourth time, and in another six weeks or so would have turned thirty-three years of age was dead.

CHAPTER II
A NEW LIFE

In those days when there were no telephones or electricity in rural areas, it still didn't take long for the news to spread and within a few hours Wally's older brother, Edwin, who was a farmer also and lived a few miles away, was appointed to be the bearer of the news to his youngest brother's new widow and her three children.

Call it premonition. Call it thought transfer. Call it E.S.P.—whatever you wish. But when Edna saw Uncle Ed coming up the pathway to the house, she knew! And before he could say a word she spoke. "Is it Walter?—Is he—Is he dead?" And wonderful Uncle Ed, with his brusk, crisp voice now broken, tearfully said, "Yes. Wally's dead."

By now relatives from both Edna's and Wally's families were arriving in their old isinglass-windowed and open cars to help in whatever ways they could.

Funeral arrangements had to be made, and the railroad company had graciously and generously agreed to pay the funeral expenses. (Please forgive the sarcasm of sixty-four years of resentment for the loss of a father I would never know in the physical sense.)

By today's standards, the little Cameron family might have become multi-millionaires as a result of such a tragedy, and such blatant negligence that caused it; but in 1927 things were different. Wally's co-workers were told to keep their mouths shut if they valued their jobs. The men told Edna of this, as they came to our little home to view the body and pay their last respects.

Tuesday Wally was laid out in the living room area of the tiny home, and the funeral was set for Wednesday afternoon. The

4

procession would travel the twenty miles to Grandview Cemetery in Johnstown, Pennsylvania, but Edna would not be there to witness the burial ceremony because the signs of the imminent coming of the new life into the world were beginning to manifest themselves.

Early Wednesday morning the three children were sent off to several neighbors and relatives for the day, as it was not deemed a good thing for children to witness such events—the funeral of their father and the birth of a new baby brother taking place simultaneously in adjacent rooms of their cottage.

Through the night and early hours of Wednesday morning the pangs of childbirth prevailed over the grief of widowhood and Edna was being tended by an old friend, Mrs. Richey, (whose son Russell would forty-three years later become Edna's third husband) and Doctor Prudeaux, who had driven up from Twin Rocks to deliver the baby.

The cars were already filling up the half-mile-long lane that led from the house out to the gravel road, and at around 8:30 A.M. Edna delivered her baby. Doctor Prudeaux lifted the child, slapped him on the posterior and got no response. Noticing the bluish skin color and lack of breathing, he laid the baby down beside Edna and said, "I'm sorry, but your baby is dead. I'll have to devote all my time to looking after you now."

After several minutes of tending to Edna, there suddenly came a squeal and the baby cried out. Now all attention was paid to the new arrival, who entered the world in such a dramatic way, and who would be named Walter, after his father, who's name was Albert Waldo, and Edwin after the family minister, and after his wonderful Uncle Ed.

After a while Edna was able to be helped to the next room for a brief last goodbye look at her beloved Walter, lying in his casket a proud new father of a not-so-bouncing baby boy.

There were over seventy-five old cars in that funeral procession —quite a spectacle, even in that day, as they drove the twenty miles to Johnstown, then snaked their way up the cemetery road which was a long series of switchback curves up the hillside to the cemetery in Westmont. So ended the life of Wally (Albert Waldo Cameron) and so began the life of Wally (Walter Edwin Cameron) on May 11, 1927.

CHAPTER III
EDNA'S STRUGGLE

Now a new day dawned and over the next few weeks Edna had some heavy decisions to make. There was no cash settlement, no windfall and no income. State widows' compensation would pay a small amount—about eight dollars per month for each child under age sixteen—and that would start in a few months, when the red tape was cut through. But for now, what to do?

The farm was actually a section of the family farm owned by Wally's grandfather Findlay Cameron, who left it to Wally's father, William Otterbien Cameron, whom we all call Ott.

Ott lived down the lane a few hundred feet in another little cottage, several of which had been built when the farm was divided up. Edna and Ott, who of course was her father-in-law, did not see eye-to-eye on numerous matters and co-existence was out of the question. So Ott bought back Wally's section of the farm for six-hundred dollars. Edna moved her family to nearby Belsano, Pennsylvania and three years later to Johnstown, where she could more readily find work to feed her family.

Edna decided she would not remarry as long as she had children at home, for fear of the overbearing hand of a "wicked stepfather" and the subconscious fear that she may once again be exposed to such as man as was her father—in her words, a rounder and a drinker, who had deserted his family.

Edna's deep rooted Christian faith would be instilled in the children in her own way and her iron will would carry the little family through the world's worst depression.

That story is another entire book, but however meagerly at times, she did it. She was mother, father, breadwinner, housekeeper—all of it—but, by God's hand and grace, she did it. Edna finally was laid to rest beside her beloved Walter on October 6th, 1990 at the age of ninety-four years. As of this writing all four children—Robert, Edith, Dr. Charles, Ph.D. and myself,—I'm the baby brother— are still alive and well.

The transition to the role of breadwinner was really tough. Much to Edna's chagrin and disgust, rumors flew that she had received a large lump sum benefit and a large insurance policy pay off. Neither rumor was true, but the rumors had the multiple effect of drawing numerous romantic suitors, for whatever purpose, and also of making it much more difficult for her to earn money as she was: trying to sell floor wax, and Larkin's products on a door-to-door basis. A young, rather attractive, and presumed wealthy widow was a threat to all the wives in the small town of Belsano, and a challenge to all the Romeos and philanderers. This, along with the possible opportunity to acquire factory work, inspired her to move into Johnstown.

Among the children's favorite of the would-be suitors was an "old" widower by the name of "Murt Edwards," who owned one of the local general merchandise stores, and who would come calling, with his pockets loaded with goodies such as Hershey's chocolate bars and chocolate covered peanuts. Edna detested the thought of being courted by this "nice enough" old man and simply was not interested. So when Murt would come knocking on the door, Edna ordered all the children to sit still on the sofa and be quiet, thus hoping he would become discouraged and leave—but poor mother! as luck would have it, one of us would find it necessary to either cough or sneeze, or use some other clever ploy, so that mother would be embarrassed and have to answer the door—and we would get our candy.

There were some good people around then, as there always are, and one of those was Ward Adams, who ran the other, larger general merchandise store. But Ward also sold gasoline, and was the post master, and had the post office in his store.

One of my sister Edith's favorite stories is about a lovely "doll baby" on display in Ward's Store. After having admired the doll on numerous trips to the store, Edith inquired as to the price, which I believe was about $3.95 the first time Edith asked. Just about every week Edith would again ask the price, and it seemed to get lower and lower each week until it was down below one dollar. Then finally one day when Edith again was asking the price, Ward answered, "Edith, I think you really want that doll, don't you?" "I'll tell you what, Edith. I'll let you have that doll for a quarter." With that Edith proceeded to make an unauthorized entry on the family bill and was given the doll.

She now awaited the fury of a strict mother, who upon finding the unexplained expense item on the bill would "lace her real good." Edith waited and worried, but the entry was never made on the bill. Ward could never let it be said he was beginning a practice of charity. If word of that got around he would soon be bankrupt. So he had simply lowered the price and sold it to a needy little girl—and just *happened* to forget to enter it on the bill. Ward later retired and became a singing Evangelist during his last years of life, I think he understood Jesus the same way I do.

Soon after the move into Johnstown, where Edna had rented a *row apartment*—what might be called a *townhouse* today—there began to appear on our porch each day a fresh quart of milk. The first day it was not possible to do much about it, so she allowed us to use it. But she rose early the next morning intending to intercept the milkman, pay him for the quart, and tell him to leave no more, because she would not be able to pay for it. The milkman informed her that a quart of mild had been ordered for our address each day for a year, and was already paid for, and that was all he could or would tell her. We never learned who had done that, but we were able to form some pretty good ideas. Whoever it was they, in their quiet anonymity, were able to share the blessing of their kindness, because we had narrowed it down to only a half dozen or so possibilities—all of whom received the benefit of our unspoken gratitude. (But dear Miss E.K., if you are still around: I think I know where it came from. That's why I worked so hard when I finally got to your Biology class.)

Forgive me for belaboring you patient readers, but I cannot narrate a life full of experiences without at least mentioning some of the kindnesses that were extended to us in those needy times. Edna did find factory work at Sam Plotkins overall factory, and later at the National Mattress Company, so that she was able to keep the wolf away from the door. As for the kids—we didn't even know we were poor.

Sam Plotkins must have been a good man too, for I never heard mother say anything but good things about him.

CHAPTER IV
CHILDHOOD YEARS

Being a youngster I was unaware of the circumstances and really didn't understand why some families had "daddies," but ours didn't. That would come later.

I do remember that from about the age of three I was always able to reason things out in an unusual way. I seemed to "just know" answers to questions, and could regularly answer my mother's questions before she asked them. And I could often come up with inexplicable solutions to complex problems. Something seemed to just "tell me" the answer.

When I was about eight my brother Charles and I, along with another friend, were walking home from a summer swim in the municipal swimming pool, where morning swimming was free for children up to sixteen, we noticed some excitement down at the Laurel Avenue underpass, where Laurel Avenue passes under the Pennsylvania Railroads "Great Broad Way," a four-track-wide right-of-way from Pittsburgh to New York City.

The *subway*, as we called it, was a long, tunnel-like underpass perhaps 300 or more feet long which had limited head room for the new, modern semi-trucks of the thirties. A large tractor-trailer had become wedged about the center of the underpass and could not move forward or backward. When we arrived on the scene it was crowded with tow trucks, winches, fire trucks, police cars—all the trappings of an exciting time in a boy's life.

As we surveyed the problem an idea popped into my head and I called out, "Why don't you let some air out of the tires?"

I don't remember staying around to see what happened, as we had a strict mother and an appointment with lunch.

So I heard no more of it and thought no more of it—until a day or so later, when our friend who had been with us at the scene said to me, "Hey Wally, you should have told them your name so they could put it in the paper. There's a big article in the morning 'Democrat' about the little boy who figured out how to get the truck out of the tunnel, but they didn't get your name."

Years later, as an industrial engineering student in a company training program in which I was participating, I discovered that the textbook had my story written up as an example of how disinterested parties, even children, can come up with startling solutions to problems. I leapt out of my seat and excitedly proclaimed, "Hey, that's me. I was that little boy!"

Suddenly I realized, from the guffaws of laughter that I was not believed, that I might as well have been reporting a U.F.O. landing. But I knew it was true and I always will.

So this sets the stage for most of what I am about to tell you: It is true. It happened to me. I have very few, if any, witnesses and I'm sure many of you will think I am either crazy or a liar, but no matter. These are all true experiences through which I have lived.

Some will attribute them to demons, some to angels, some to spirits. I don't know. All I know is none of it has interfered with my deep and abiding love of God, and my belief that Jesus of Nazareth is the one and only Christ, the living Son of the living God, who is God, who always was and always will be.

So that is out of the way. I do not know how or why these things come about, but as to demons, well that is nonsense. Some people would slap an angel in the face out of ignorance.

Just to digress briefly and to make a subtle distinction between my Christian faith and my "mystical experiences," I feel it necessary to make this point: My mother was well-founded in her belief that "Spiritualism" (The religion) is of the devil and that anyone who delves into it will be cursed, but, at the same time, she would relate factually of mysterious happenings, one of which I somewhat recall.

Some months after Wally's death there arose a fiscal problem of some kind that required a certain document that my mother had to provide in a very important matter. It may have been an insurance policy, a tax receipt, or something else. It involved a serious family crisis if the document were not located and shown to the proper authorities. Mother had not even known of the existence of this piece

10

of paper—much less its location—so she was duly frustrated by the need to produce it.

In a dream Mother had, her departed husband, Walter, came to the foot of her bed and spoke to her, and told her precisely where to find the document. She went there and fount it, exactly as she was told she would.

Another of the stories I heard my mother tell, then I will go about the work of telling my own story.

Mother many times repeated these tales, and this once again was of a dream she had, one that curiously stuck with her and bothered her. It was about a year prior to Walter's accidental death that she dreamed of seeing a long funeral procession, moving up the side of a mountain on a winding road and she had the feeling that she belonged in that funeral procession. But for some reason, something to do with a baby, she could not be at the funeral.

Was this a prophetic foretelling of doom? Was there some purpose in this dream—or did she dig it up from her subconscious mind? Why do we need to try to explain these things anyway? Can't we just accept the fact that it happened? Then perhaps one day we might find out what causes such things, or perhaps we might not. What's the difference? My faith tells me that the infinite wisdom of God will reveal to us what we need to know—if and when we need to know it. We were created for a purpose known only to God and I'm sure God is great enough, and intelligent enough, to fulfill his own purpose without us trying to re-engineer it for him.

I had a few strange experiences at about the age of seven or so, at about the same time the first subtle twitches, muscle tics, and other nervous habits, which (we did not know at the time) were the signals of the onset of "Tourette syndrome."

This might lend some credence to the line of thinking that St. Vitus Dance people are demon-possessed, and so reinforce the medieval beliefs of some folks.

I can remember being able to see "death" on people's faces. I don't know what I saw, it was just something about their faces, and "something told me" that this person was about to die.

One very pretty little classmate of mine in second grade, a nice girl I knew only from school—she was one of about thirty-five students in the class—and I knew her only in that context.

One day as we were reporting to the playground for recess, this little girl walked past where I was standing and at that moment I saw "death" on her face.

Two weeks later I was in her home—for her funeral service. She had not been known to be ill. She had no reason for dying, at least none known to anyone in that day and age. She had simply died. I'm sure she must have had some undiagnosed illness that would not go unnoticed today. Regardless, it happened—just like that.

I saw this numerous times in older people, and sure enough, soon they would die. I have never told anyone of this, until this very moment of writing, but it happened.

I had no wish for any of these people to die. It was just some information I was being given. "Something just told me."

There was one exception to this, an exception that still bothers me somewhat. Although I'm not foolish enough to think I have enough intercessory power to bring about someone's death, this one just tingles my conscience a tiny bit when I think of it.

One block over from Laurel Avenue (where the truck got stuck in the tunnel) is Butler Avenue, where we happened to be living at this time. During the winter months, when the snow was just right, the City of Johnstown Parks and Recreation Department would block off, to traffic, certain streets and permit *coasting* or sled riding. Butler Avenue was such a street, and known to be one of the very best because of its long, gradual slope, and nice level run-out at the end, as well as a cold running stream to plunge into if you had too fast a sled.

We all loved to sled ride every evening until whatever time our respective parents required us at home.

There was one particular "Bully" who was about fifteen years old and who would not ride a sled but rather insisted on wearing skates.

This bully would pick on the smaller children; he loved to skate in front of them and lift one skate off the ice and flash it at them as though he were going to cut them. All of us smaller children were scared to death of him and he loved it. He seemed to enjoy scaring us and would take over the hill until we all went home.

He loved to be king of the hill and would gleefully skate around all alone, while we only watched. He knew we were afraid of him and we knew what he would do if we rode our sleds.

I remember vividly wishing him dead. *I wish he would die so we could ride our sleds in peace,* I thought. I never remember seeing "death" on his face, but I do remember ever so vividly in late winter or early spring, standing in the living room of his home, feeling mixed emotions of relief from the teasing that would be no more, and guilt and a sense of loss, while I stood there viewing his body in its casket. And I remember his mother's painful screams, "My baby, my baby! Why God, why did you take my baby?"

I then realized that this terrible bully, too, was loved dearly, and was a mother's treasure also. Why had she not told him to behave and not be such a bully?

I still remember his nickname. But I would not dare to relate even that because I'm sure there are people today who still miss that young man and I bear no ill will, just a child's-eye memory of a childhood terror.

This I firmly believe to be just a coincidence, and nothing more, but it was something that did happen.

CHAPTER V
SOME CHRISTMASES

Without a doubt, Christmas season was my favorite time of the year.

Our mama knew how to set her priorities, as well as how to manage the household finances. By this I mean she knew how to arrange things so that we would have something for Christmas.

There were some lean years for this widowed mother, scraping to raise four kids through the depths of the great depression and 1934 was probably the leanest, at least the leanest that I can remember. It is, no doubt, for that very reason that it stands out as one of the best Christmases ever.

There were some years that were so lean that buying a Christmas tree was out of the question, so we had to resort to using the little artificial tree that was still left over from better times. Other years we would be able to buy a small, "table-top" live cut tree for as little as ten cents.

I seem to remember 1934 as being one of those ten-cent-tree years. In any event, I do know we had a short tree that year, probably less than three feet tall.

Bob, my oldest brother, would have been seventeen that year, so he took charge of the Christmas tree project.

He mounted the small tree on a fruit crate—probably a grape crate, as that would be about the right size and shape to fit my memory of it. He then, after setting the tree where and how he wanted it, covered the grape crate with an old sheet. We all lamented how nice it would be if we could afford the luxury of putting artificial grass, and a little village under the tree. We also knew that we had no materials to provide such a luxury, and no money to buy them.

Always tenacious at the thought of a good idea, I pressed on with it.

"We could put some sand down for a little road, and I could put my toy cowboy on horseback on the road," I suggested. Charles said, "I can put my toy car on the road, and maybe we can make some fences and things like that with toothpicks on little sticks." "Yeah! And we could get some sticks up in the hills and make a little log cabin," someone, perhaps it was Edith, suggested.

"Okay," said Bob, "We'll go up into the hills and see what we can find."

So off we went, up into the beautiful mountainous forest, like those that surround every city and town in Pennsylvania, wielding baskets, buckets and a little coal shovel. We rolled up large mats of lush, green ground moss, found all the "just right" sticks we needed for a log cabin, got a bucket of white sand out of the creek bottom and headed for home.

Happy hours were devoted to spreading the moss into a lush carpet of imaginary grass; which was mounded up over the grape crate tree base to form a neat little hill effect. Next we decided on a route for our white sand road, while somebody, probably Charles, built the log cabin.

Now, with the tree all trimmed, the lights beaming a happy birthday greeting to our Savior, and our little homemade scene under the tree we all just relaxed and enjoyed the fruits of our happy labors. Someone even dropped one of the tree lights strings down low enough so we could put a light in our cabin, and pretend the adjacent lights were street lights. It was a great time and the best viewing was from flat on your back on the floor.

Santa brought me a twenty-five-cent toy Greyhound "semi" tour bus—a replica of the trams used at the 1933 Chicago World's Fair—and a fifty-cent cast-iron car hauler truck.

There is no fonder memory in my "total recall" repertoire.

One thing we always had in abundance was popcorn or, more accurately, "popping corn, since several of our relatives were farmers, who raised the corn on their farms."

New Year's Eve that same year was a real Huckleberry Finn and Tom Sawyer type occasion as it turned out.

Charles, about eleven or twelve years old, and I, at seven years old, were to stay at home alone. Mother and Edith had gone to "Watch night" service at church, and Bob had gone out with the "guys."

The two stay-homers were given permission to stay up to ring in the new year before going to bed.

After tiring of sitting around looking at our now, two-week-old Christmas tree (we always set our tree up a week before Christmas), we decided to pop some corn. We would pop it so it could be strung on the Christmas tree—why not, since we always left our tree up until "Greek Christmas" anyway.

We would have to sugar-coat the popcorn and since Charles knew how to do that, we started. We popped corn, and mixed sugar coating. We filled the dishpan with white sugar-coated popcorn enjoying the eating of it as we "worked"—or I should say, played.

We still had a large bowl of liquified sugar left over, so Charles said, "Wally, you make some more popcorn while I put some red food coloring in the sugar coating, and we can make red popcorn too."

Well, needless to say, I popped too much corn, and we now had the other dishpan, the drying pan, filled with popcorn, with some left over. So, we made some green sugar coating.

By the time mother and the rest of the family arrived home there were two sick little boys zonked out in front of the Christmas tree, and in the kitchen, filling the table was a dishpan full of red popcorn, a dishpan full of white popcorn, a turkey roaster top, full of green popcorn, and a turkey roaster bottom full of butter and salt popcorn; with all the necessary accompanying dirty dishes and utensils. Even though we had used up all the powdered sugar in the house Mama was lenient and saw the humor of the situation—and Charles and I groaned a relieved sigh as Bob, Edith and Mama all dug into the special New Year's treat we had prepared.

The next year, Christmas of 1935, we had again moved to another house, a few blocks away from the popcorn episode house. I was now eight years old and having serious doubts about the reality of Santa Claus. We had already deposed the Easter Bunny, and that was all right with me because, frankly, I never really bought into a large, person-sized rabbit, hopping around with sacks full of jelly beans and chocolate. Now Santa Claus—that was another matter: you could go downtown and talk to him at the stores, and he was a real person, like Jesus was a real person. So I did not want to let go of Santa Claus—even though all my friends now teased me for still wanting to believe. Well, any doubts I may have had were wiped out for at least another year on Christmas Eve of 1935.

Mama was the youth director of the Garfield Street Evangelical Church, and she had arranged for the youth group to go carolling on Christmas Eve. Charles and I would go carolling with mama and Bob would go with the young adult men's group. Edith had already left home and was living in another town.

We left to assemble at the church right after supper, thence to go carolling, and then to meet at Mrs. Given's house for refreshments and a Christmas Eve party.

It was one of the most beautiful winter nights ever, with about six or more inches of freshly fallen snow on the ground on a bright moonlit, starry night. The snow crunched under foot in the near ten-degree weather.

I paid particular attention that everything was normal at home as we departed; there were no signs of impending Christmas other than the already decorated tree.

It occurred to me that if any family member was going to play Santa, he or she would have to do it after I got back home and was in bed, since we were all out together. Bob already had left for the church before we left the house, so his doing it was out of the question. I had them now, I thought, saying not a word to a soul. If I got back home and everything was just as we left it, I would know; Santa is a fake. But on the other hand—well, we just would wait and see.

It was a marvelous time—song books, a trumpet player, and several other musicians added to the musical quality of the event.

We sang and played carols in front of as many parishioners' homes as we could reasonably get to. I so very vividly remember singing "It Came Upon a Midnight Clear" in front of Mrs. Winstanley's house. I sang extra loudly because Mrs. Winstanley's daughter, Dora, was my Sunday school teacher and I wanted her to hear me.

It was getting colder and later the snow on the heavily travelled streets was packed hard and glazing over. People were getting out their sleighs and horses and were riding up and down Fairfield Avenue, with the sleigh bells jingling.

The Givens lived on Fairfield Avenue and so did Winstanleys; so that was our last, latest and coldest stop before walking down to the party at the Givens' home.

We welcomed the hot chocolate and cookies that were served immediately upon our arrival; then we laughed, talked, sang and marveled at the beautiful sound of the sleigh bells still jingling up and down Fairfield Avenue.

We partied on until 2:00 A.M., before finally breaking up and heading homeward.

It took nearly a half hour to get home, with Bob making some sage comments along the way home about my probably being missed by Santa Claus, since I had not been home. I knew he was teasing; that didn't really bother me. What was bothering me was logistics; how were they going to pull this off in the event I was mistaken about there being a real Santa Claus?

All my fears and questions were answered as we entered our house at 2:30 A.M. Christmas morning. There in front of the Christmas tree were all my gifts—and a lengthy note from Santa, explaining that he knew why I was not in bed.

Even the annual Christmas treat plates were set out as always: a picnic plate, complete with name tags, for each of us—with the usual orange, puffed rice ball, hard tack candy, mixed nuts in the shells, and always a little circus box full of chocolate drops.

I was totally convinced. There was *no way* they could have pulled that off, short of Santa Claus really being Santa Claus.

And nobody in the family has ever yet told me how they did it. Once I asked Bob if he had a hand in it and he wisely answered, "You mean you still don't believe in Santa Claus?" And that wasn't too many years ago.

CHAPTER VI
1938 THE KEYSTONE YEAR

In 1938 we moved from the Morrellville-Oakhurst area of Johnstown to Kernville, a mixed residential/commercial area, closer to downtown Johnstown, and closer to the mattress factory where Mother worked.

It was a significant move, since it was ten or twelve miles distance and meant all new schools, friends, churches, neighbors and even a new need to learn where all the best shops were.

Before we moved to Kernville, I had known Dave Penrod, who was my very best friend in the whole world. We were together most of the time. I even had supper at his house frequently, to minimize the interruptions of our playtime. But about a year or more earlier, Dave's family had moved far away to another place, somewhere halfway across town, and I never saw him again. He is the first person I ever recall caring so much about that I really missed him and was deeply hurt by not having him as a friend any longer.

We now moved to Kernville, into half of a huge, three-story sid-by-side duplex, or *double house*, on Franklin Street. The main streetcar line ran on Franklin Street, so it was busy, noisy, and very convenient. The house was large enough so that mother could sub-let two apartments and reserve the second floor for our family.

On my first excursion around the neighborhood to seek new friends I got the most pleasant and shocking surprise of my life— right there in the alley behind our house (Thomas Avenue), was a group of kids my age playing—and what to my wondering eyes should appear, but a little old friend I held so dear.

There was Dave Penrod and —wonder of wonders—we now lived about one hundred and fifty feet apart as the crow flies. I now had lost any and all trepidations and fears of the new neighborhood and was totally delighted. I ran home to tell Mama of my discovery. She never told me that she had already known about it and was just waiting for me to discover it.

I guess you could call the two years we lived in that building a keystone in my young life, for so many good things happened to me during that time. One of the good things was that my older brother and his wife were the first renters and moved into the first-floor apartment. Bob now had a good job at the Open Hearth Furnace Department of Bethlehem Steel Company, which was one of the largest employers in the area.

That's where Charles got his first bicycle, and I my first wagon—a nice, wooden wagon with removable, red stake-board sides. And that's where I got my Lionel electric train on Christmas of 1938. And that's where I got my Introduction into the World of Earning Money.

A boy about one year older than I (who was called "Whitey" because of his towheaded hair color) lived around the corner from us.

Whitey also had a wagon and we became fairly good friends. I learned that on Saturdays, Whitey "rented out" his wagon to one of the clerks at the A&P store across the street, for fifty cents a day. The clerk would then use the wagon to deliver groceries to store customers. The new young manager, Bill Sweeney, was very enterprising and would accept phone-in grocery lists, and would fill order lists dropped off by customers and the clerk would load the orders onto Whitey's wagon and deliver them to the customer's home.

One Saturday morning our doorbell rang and when I answered it, there stood the A&P clerk. He said, "Can I borrow your wagon? Whitey's wagon is broken and can't be fixed. I'll pay you fifty cents." *Fifty Cents!* "Well," I said, "All right—if you're sure it's okay with Whitey." He reassured me and I let him have my wagon, but I never got the fifty cents. The next Saturday he was back again needing the wagon, but I said, "No, you can't have it. You promised to pay me fifty cents and you didn't, so you can't use my wagon"

About an hour or so later the doorbell rang again. This time it was Bill Sweeney at the door. (At that time I had rather white hair also.)

Bill said "Whitey, if you will bring your wagon over, and deliver some groceries for me, I'll pay you sixty cents and you can keep the tips you get, as well.

Well, you can bet we signed an old fashioned contract with a "word of bond," and I was on my way.

The A&P store was not a supermarket; it was what they called a "counter store." It had a grocery counter, a meat counter, a produce counter, and a notions counter where the coffee, tea, butter, candy, gum etc. was sold. The customers would line up at whichever of the counters and wait to be served and the clerks would go get the merchandise from the shelves for them—no self service—so the waiting was long and tiresome, and thus was Bill Sweeney's order filling service a success.

I hauled groceries all day and in between I broke down bread boxes for return, sacked potatoes into peck bags, stocked shelves and whatever else I was able to do. All this was illegal, so it was kept very much under cover—except for the delivery wagon. In the middle of the back room was the produce cooler, a room-sized walk-in refrigerator, which was about eight feet high. The top of the cooler was a good place to store the empty cardboard boxes used for the delivery orders.

It also made for a good hiding place for me to scoot into if a company official should happen to make a surprise Saturday visit, for if I were caught working there at age eleven, Bill Sweeney would be fired immediately.

We had signals worked out so I would know when to hide—or when to act like just another customer, if I happened to come back from a delivery while we had "unwelcome" visitors.

My sixty cents soon was raised to eighty cents and then to a dollar. My tips usually exceeded my wages. The best part was after closing time Saturday evening, when Bill would set aside such things as doughnuts, bananas, pound cakes, bread, and so forth, that could not be held over for sale the next week. So each Saturday I would go home with a wagon load of groceries and "Doc" the butcher would see to it that we got a good portion of high-grade beef to fill the order of fifteen or twenty cents worth that mother usually requested.

I kept that Saturday job for three years, along with a newspaper route I acquired at age twelve. Then Bill was transferred to a brand new Supermarket and Jimmy Fockler, who had been the produce manager, took Bill's place as manager. Jimmy was a really great guy, who always treated me well. He was a very devoted member of the Jehovah's Witness faith. Not being comfortable with the "illegitimate" employee, his first act was to fire me and my heart was broken.

I'm not sure where Jesus stands on some of these "moral principle" decisions, but Jimmy was doing what he knew to be the right thing.

The timing was pretty good because my so called "illness" began soon after the firing, so I would not have been able to work anyway.

Meanwhile, mother would grocery shop at Bill Sweeney's new store and he never failed to inquire about me.

After my recuperation period, Bill Sweeney told Mother to have "Whitey" apply for working papers and get a social security card and he would have a job for me. Bill Sweeney and little "Whitey" had a mutual respect for each other that would be hard to top. Bill had even on a few occasions given me the weeks "take" in a bank bag, placed in a brown grocery bag and had me deliver it to the bank. I learned later that I had been followed by a security guard and that the purpose was to avoid the possibility of Bill being robbed, as he feared might happen. So the innocent little kid was the "real messenger" and the manager was a decoy—very interesting. But that is just to point out the trust Bill placed in me, and I in him.

I got my working papers and a special school permit. Since I was an honors student, I could have Tuesday and Friday afternoons off school. So, along with Saturday, that made a nifty work week for a high school freshman and sophomore. Summertime brought full-time work and the bananas, doughnuts, bread, and so on still continued at the supermarket.

Now, there was a rule at our house—an Edict from Edna—*Any money that comes into this house will be given to Edna.* She would count it and give half back to the presenter. Edna's half was for room and board, or "keep" as she called it. Our half was for whatever we wanted to do with it. Any clothing we bought, however, was paid for equally between our own money and mother's. We all thought it was a pretty good arrangement, but I was always trying to get "cash credit" for extra grocery goodies I brought home. It never worked; we just split the cash down the middle. I stayed at the store and was dedicated to my job and to Bill Sweeney—until I left him to go to Ohio.

I would like nothing better than to hear from Bill Sweeney if he still lives—or from any of my co-workers at that best ever A&P Supermarket.

CHAPTER VII
SKIPPY

Probably the best day in that banner year of 1938 was the day I got my first dog.

I couldn't believe it. Are my eyes deceiving me—or *do I really see Mama carrying a puppy?* I had always anxiously awaited Mama's arrival home from her factory job, for she often had a little surprise— sometimes those super delicious raisin-filled "bar cookies" that the bakery man brought for the factory vending machines, sometimes a candy bar. (Bit-O-Honey was Mama's favorite, so we occasionally were treated to one also.) But on this day—a puppy. "Can it really be true?" I asked. "Yes," said Mama, "I've brought you a puppy. One of the men at the factory had brought it to work, in the hope of finding a new home for him."

He was about four months old already, and was over the "fuzz-ball" puppy stage; he was beginning to look like a dog.

I named him "Pal" because my friend Dave Penrod once had a dog named Pal—and that was good enough for me.

Pal was a mixed breed, but was mainly what we called a "toy collie."

He had a medium-length, golden bronze hair, four white paws, and a black face with a perfect white divider stripe down the center of his nose. He also had perfect black eyebrows over each eye. His most prized possession was his beautiful "flag tail," that curled up over his back in a crescent shape, with a long golden mane-like hair standing straight and proud, out from that crescent tail. Below the tail, on his rear quarter, he had a pair of golden cushions, which, like his tail, gave him a look of elegant distinction.

He was a very smart dog, easy to train and housebreak, and he loved to please us.

Charles and I argued over who's dog Pal was meant to be, but I knew he was mine.

One day Charles and I were taking him for a walk on Franklin Street—on a leash of course—and Charles decided to unleash him. I pleaded, "Please don't let him loose. There is too much traffic. He'll run out in the street and get killed!" Charles didn't think he would run out into the street, so he let him loose.

Immediately Pal ran out into the street and was running around like wild, enjoying his newly found freedom.

I screamed as Pal darted between the cars, when suddenly he ran directly in front of an oncoming streetcar. I watched in horror as the "cow catcher" of the speeding trolley car caught my little dog and sent him flying and tumbling, end over end, about ten feet into the air. He landed on the street on all four feet, going full speed ahead; he dashed in front of the streetcar narrowly missing being hit a second time, and made a bee line to where we were standing on the sidewalk.

He was terrified, "piddling" all over the sidewalk and shaking like a leaf—but he was unhurt and I felt like the resurrection had reoccurred.

I forgot to explain how Pal became Skippy. One day I was holding Pal in my lap on the front porch steps, when a neighbor from across the street came walking past. When she saw my dog she said, "Hello Skippy." and Pal jumped from my arms and began to dance and cavort with obvious joy. The lady then explained that she was a friend of the folks who had owned "Skippy" before. She was quite upset because she had been trying to obtain "Skippy" for herself but the owners would not hear of it, because she lived on such a dangerous street, and now—here was Skippy—living across the street from her. She said to me, "You have a very nice little dog. Take care of him and if you ever want to find him a new home, please—please bring him to me."

So Pal became Skippy—and he seemed to be a much happier dog now that I knew his proper name.

After the streetcar incident, Skippy never needed a leash again. He never went into the street, and as true as I sit here, if he ever decided to cross the street he would go to the crosswalk at the intersection, wait for traffic, look both ways, and safely cross the street.

We moved from the big Franklin Street house to Sherman Street, a few blocks away. Sherman Street was cut into the side of a large hill, and the house towered above the street. It was, again, a double house, and had a high retaining wall from the street level up to the front yard level. The wall must have been at least eight feet high on the neighbors' side of the house. There was a small lawn between the wall and the two levels of porches the house possessed.

One day the neighbors in the adjacent house were entertaining guests on the upper-level front porch. Skippy knew there were strangers up there, so he went over on the neighbors' side of the lawn, stood up on his hind feet and began voicing his disapproval of the strangers on the porch. He kept looking up at the porch, staying up on his hind legs to get as near to the problem as possible, barking and barking. He was unaware that he was "walking backwards" while on two feet and barking, he backed right off the edge of the high wall. Once again he hit the bricks at full speed, yelping and racing up the concrete steps to where we were on our lower porch, leaving a wet line behind him as he piddled up the stairs. And don't think dogs have no sense of reason or emotion—Skippy was visibly embarrassed.

Skippy soon learned of Mama's after-work treats too, so he developed the habit of waiting inside the kitchen door each day at five o'clock.

Skippy was an outside/inside dog, and much to Mama's chagrin, I allowed him to run loose around the neighborhood. He had his regular routes to cover, but he never abused the privilege and was always, I mean *always*, at that kitchen door at five o'clock to greet Mama.

One morning while on her way to leaving for work, Mama slipped and fell down the long flight of concrete steps to the street. She tore her left kidney loose and had to be hospitalized for about five weeks.

Every working day, Monday through Friday, of those five weeks Skippy kept his daily vigil. He would sit by that kitchen door and wait. At about a quarter to six or six o'clock he would whimper a little "cry" and leave his post to make his appointed rounds. On Saturday or Sunday, he didn't wait for her; somehow he knew these things.

When Mama finally came home, she was not able to walk without assistance, so two men (I don't know if they were Mama's friends from the factory, or if they were hospital orderlies) brought her home in a car and proceeded to support her on both sides while they climbed the three full flights of stairs to her bedroom. Skippy watched dutifully as the men helped her from the car. He followed closely behind, tail wagging, as they scaled the three flights of stairs. Down the hall to the back bedroom and into the room, with Skippy still only a half step behind.

The moment those two men sat Mother into her bed and took their hands off her, Skippy went into action.

The hair on his back bristled, he bared his teeth, growled the most menacing warning I had ever heard, and proceeded to run those two poor guys back down the three flights of stairs at a pace you would not believe—all the time nipping and snapping at their heels and letting them know in no uncertain terms that nobody was ever going to take Mama away again while Skippy had any say in the matter. Still, he had been wise enough to be ever so tolerant until Mama was safely in her bed.

Skippy became more protective of the household after that and since Mama was once again sub-letting parts of the huge house, his protectiveness became his downfall. Mama would not tolerate having the tenants' guests frightened by the dog. So, on the saddest day of my life, Skippy was given to my Uncle Blair, who lived in the country.

I don't think Mama had any idea what she did to me, and to Charles, when she gave Skippy away. If she had, she never would have done it. Poor Skippy was the victim of his own great love and devotion to our Mama.

The last time I ever saw Sippy was another testimony to that great dog's devotion and obedience.

One Sunday my friend "Jimbo" Collins and I were out riding our bicycles. We liked to take long, long bike rides. So on this day we headed out in the direction of Uncle Blair's house, probably thirteen miles or so away.

When Jimbo and I arrived, there was nobody at home—but there was Skippy, out in the yard, guarding the property.

When he saw me, he immediately went on a tear, as fast as he could run, around the house, then over to me, and around the house again. It seemed like ten minutes before Skippy settled down enough so I could pet him and visit with him. You can bet I got my ears and face washed with his flying tongue. I guess we stayed about half an hour, until I decided we would have to leave. As we remounted our bicycles, Skippy decided he was going to tag along, as he so often had done before. No matter how fast I would go, Skippy would be out there in front of me, running interference.

But this time I knew it could not be; every bone in my body ached. Every fibre of my being was screaming at me to let him come along, but I knew it was only a dream, that Mama would give me "what for" and ship Skippy right back out here—or worse.

While straddling my bicycle, I performed the most difficult act of obedience I would ever be called on to perform—and so did my dearly beloved Skippy. I looked him in the eyes, my own eyes now filled with tears, and pointing my finger at his nose, said, "Skippy, stay." Skippy cocked his head right, then left, while sitting in his "Stay" position.

Jimbo and I rode off, and as far as I could see, before we turned onto the highway, Skippy was obediently sitting there, head cocked inquisitively as I rode out of his life forever.

Skippy was once more transferred to another uncle's home, farther away. One fine day, while I was serving in the U.S. Navy, Skippy was killed in action.

He had been protecting his household against the intrusion of a huge doberman, or some similar large dog, and he lost his life while doing the only thing that ever mattered to Skippy—protecting his master's property.

I am pleased to tell you that in my experiences, I have found out that people are rejoined with their faithful dogs in the next world. So, God bless you, Skippy—and keep watching the gates—one fine day, I'll be there to greet you again.

CHAPTER VIII
THE LONG ILLNESS

In September of 1941, Mother decided I must have some health problem and so she made an appointment with the doctor who had cared for her after her fall.

His diagnosis was that I had contracted a form of rheumatic fever call "rheumatic chorea."

This was, he thought, the cause of my many muscular tics, grunting noises, and excessive throat clearing and sniffling. It had some resemblance to Huntington chorea, and was accompanied by a heart murmur. He also knew that I had a long history of serious sore throat episodes, some of which were quinsy (or tonsillitis), others of which were strep throat.

All of this did subject me to some forms of discrimination, as I was frequently made to sit out in the hall at school for not being able to stop my throat clearing, grunting and squirming.

I was hospitalized, and soon lost my appendix and tonsils. They kept me in the hospital for ten weeks—and bedfast at home for a year. I missed my ninth grade in high school—and never once felt "sick." My bed wetting stopped forever while I was in the hospital, but the twitching never did.

Many people believed (and still do) that people with St. Vitus Dance are demon-possessed. That would fit right in with any psychic abilities I may possess along the way.

Today I know that what I always had was Tourette's syndrome. I had spent a year of my life, wasting time in bed and losing a year of school—for nothing. I never had rheumatic chorea or rheumatic fever. I had a serious case of improper diagnosis; years and years would elapse before medical science recognized Tourette's syndrome, a disease discovered in France by Dr. Gilles De La Tourette during the nineteenth century, but still shrouded with a suspicion and mysticism a hundred years later. Thank God, for the thousands of children afflicted with this horrible nightmare, that there is progress and some hope today which did not exist too few years ago.

Well, to climax this chapter—during the time of my "illness," while semi-bedfast at home, I was not permitted to climb stairs, so arrangements had to be made for me to live on one floor lest I should drop dead of a heart attack (I say with some sarcasm). But, anyway we all believed it, so we followed the doctor's rules to the letter.

At the time we lived in one of those Pennsylvania hillside homes, with two-level front porches and two flights of steps up to the back porch and kitchen. The kitchen was at ground level at the rear of the house; the living room was two flights up from the street at the front of the house. There was no ingress or egress to the street from the rear; it was all fenced in by neighboring backyards, so the only way in or out was "down front." Needless to say, being restricted to one floor, I stayed at home.

But when Christmastime approached, Charles and I got itchy. It was time to go shopping for a Christmas tree, to get out the trains (I had one and he had one), and to make our annual layout under the Christmas tree—complete with miniature village, houses, roads, animals, etc. We loved it.

We just *had* to go out Christmas tree shopping. At this time I was fourteen years old and Charles just turned nineteen. I was no small child, having grown over three inches during the course of nine months or so of "illness;" but Charles agreed to carry me piggy-back, down to the street, where we could get into his 1930 Model "A" Ford, which we called the "little drop of wine." It was a rumble seat coupe, which he bought for thirty dollars and painted a vivid wine color—thus the name.

Now we are coming to the "corny" part of the story but it is true, true, true—and as vivid in my memory as if it happened this afternoon. However you are not going to believe it because what I am about to tell you supposedly happened in Korea years later—and maybe it did. But it also happened to me-or Charles—in 1941 before Christmas.

As Charles reached the street-level sidewalk, after struggling to carry me piggy-back down the two flights of stairs, and just as he was about to set me down so we could get into the car, a man walked past, and wanting to make some comment as to the situation, the man said, "That's quite a load you've got there." Charles replied, "He's not heavy; he's my brother." With that the man smiled, shook his head and repeated, " 'He's not heavy; he's my brother.' Wow, isn't that something."

I assure you before Almighty God, and all that is holy, that is exactly what happened—and the way it happened. Charles says he doesn't really remember the incident. So, okay, it doesn't matter. I know and God knows it happened—and if it happened again somewhere else, to somebody else, then that's great because that's how and why God made brothers—and I'm sure any brother, anywhere, in the world would do the same thing.

P.S. We got a wonderful tree that year. Johnstown High School won the WPIAL Football Championship. It was a good year.

CHAPTER IX
OHIO AND PEGGY

Another year went by and the War raged on. Charles, now working in a prestigious men's clothing store and approaching destiny's date with the draft board, enlisted in the Army Air Corps as an aviation cadet. While working at the clothing store he met Marian Ganoe who was to become his wife and who, coincidentally, lived in the house almost directly adjacent to the rear of our place. So it was just Mama and me—Edna and Wally. (Is that irony or what?)

I worked part-time at the A&P (since I had now "recovered" from my "serious" illness and attended Joseph Johns Junior High School, from which I would graduate tenth grade a year later, in 1944.

Summer vacation came and with it the prospect of longer hours at the supermarket. But I was getting antsy. I had heard about the war plants in Ohio, with their long hours and high wages—and my sister, now a mother of two girls, lived near Warren, Ohio. Her husband had a very good job as supervisor in a large war plant, where they built LCM landing barges, and large diesel engines for cargo and warships, where I figured he could get me a job.

I quit the A&P, left Mama, and went to spend the summer in Ohio—making big money.

When September approached, Sis and I talked of the possibility of me staying on and going to Newton Falls High School, where Sis agreed to sign for me to play football. I knew mama would never allow me to play football because of my "terrible illness" and there was no greater love in my life then football, so I stayed.

Being the bashful boy that I was made me not too prominent in the social set. Football practice and church attendance were compulsory, so my time for socializing was limited.

I noticed this beautiful, petite blonde who was in my Speech class, English class and homeroom. She was so beautiful. She looked like a movie star, and to my good fortune, she occupied the seat behind me in one of those classes. We talked and I found her very easy to talk with and friendly to me. Just a nice person—and beautiful. I never would have presumed to think she may have been interested in me other than conversationally, because she was just too high-class and beautiful for anyone as ordinary as me.

Football season ended; holiday season was approaching. I got to play in several games and the coach even told me he was looking forward to next year—when I would be first string.

Praise God! Hallelujah! Wow! But it was not to be.

One day in class the beautiful little blonde, Peggy Bailey, handed me a neatly folded note, which I didn't open until I arrived home at my Sis's house after school. The note read:

> Dear Wally:
>
> There is going to be a Christmas dance at the Community Center on Saturday, December (whatever) I would like to go to the dance and would be very pleased if you would agree to escort me.
>
> Yours Truly,
> Peg Bailey

Wow! What brought this on? I wondered. Of course I agreed, but first I had to check around and see if she was really all right. Everyone of my friends said I was a lucky guy and that she was a great gal.

But a little later, after a few dates when the church folk became aware that I was "going with" Peggy Bailey, well, some of them thought they'd better tell me: The Bailey family members are Spiritualists, and you know, that is of the devil.

Now what should I do. I simply could not get serious with a girl who was a Spiritualist.

I didn't really know what a Spiritualist was, but I knew it wasn't good and it wouldn't set well with my upbringing and my own Christian ideals. So I decided to do the right thing and just plain out ask her. So one nice sunny day we were seated on a park bench on the town square, by the ever-present town cannon and hero statue, when I brought up the subject. "Peggy, I've got something very serious and important to ask you," I said. And in her lovely and demure way, she replied, "Well, okay, what is it?" I squirmed a little, and hem-hawed a little, and then indiscreetly blurted out, "I hear you are a Spiritualist. Is that true?"

She knew if she answered, "Yes, it's true," it would be all over—and it really wasn't true in the real, technical sense. So, she told me the one and only "little white lie" I have ever heard her utter.

"No, I'm not a Spiritualist, I go to the Congregational Church over there," she said as she pointed diagonally across the intersection to the stately edifice.

I sort of knew it wasn't the whole truth—but I didn't want to hear anymore. I was in love for life and I knew it. And anyway, it seemed the Lord had made it my mission to save her soul and redeem her from a certain destiny in Hell. Anyway, nobody so lovely, so nice could ever not go to Heaven. I allowed myself then to crash down full force in the deepest chasm of young love.

Just about Christmastime some more excitement developed. Sis's doctor told her she "must" move to Arizona for her health, or she would not live much longer. So the house was sold, Sis and her family purchased a long "house trailer" and car to pull it, and were heading for Arizona.

Now what was I to do, soon to be eighteen years old, and now kicked back another year in school. Arizona was out of the question for me and going back to Johnstown—where the school was so much more advanced and so much larger—I just couldn't possibly make it. Anyway, they were now drafting eighteen-year-olds, who were either graduates or drop outs from high school. So I moved myself back to Johnstown and enlisted in the Navy, in Combat Air Crew Service, and waited to be called to active duty.

At just about the time I was to report for duty, Charles was coming home from overseas,having completing fifty bombing missions as a B-24 pilot, flying from Italy and North Africa. Bob the oldest, was now almost twenty-eight and was threatened by the draft. He also had entered the Air Corps and was commissioned as a bombardier-navigator. He was too old for pilot training at that age so he served as an instructor at Williams Air Base, in Mesa, Arizona, just three or four miles from where I'm now sitting in our retirement home.

After a year and a half, I was discharged from the Navy, in August 1946, and subsequently went back to Ohio to look for work—and to see my Peggy, with whom my love affair was no less intense and who now was reigning Homecoming Queen.

CHAPTER X
THE ELOPEMENT

Peg and I had really only a few short months to enjoy each other's company before Sis's move to Arizona interrupted my life. So we had conducted a postal service romance all during my Navy time and afterward, until I finally returned to Newton Falls, Ohio about February of 1947.

I rented a sleeping room from a very nice older couple in the little village of Newton Falls and was lucky enough to find a fairly good job with Youngstown Kitchens, then called Mullins Manufacturing Company in Warren, Ohio. There was regular bus service between Newton Falls, Warren, and Youngstown, so transportation was not a problem, a little inconvenient perhaps, but not a problem.

Peg was now enrolled at Youngstown College School of Business (now Youngstown State University), and beginning in September, would be living in a girls' dorm on campus. However, she would be at home most or all of the summer and we would be able to date. Things were very nice—very nice, that is, until Peg's parents decided she was getting too "serious" with this uneducated young vagabond, of whom they had decided to not approve. It was all for her best interest, of course, as she certainly was too young at eighteen years to get too serious—and they had plans for her to find a much more promising young man than I appeared to be. So they issued an order to Peg: *You will stop seeing this young man.* Period. Peg told me of the order, a watered down version, to be sure. She also told me that she fully intended to keep right on seeing me, but I would not be able to call on her at home.

In other words, we would have to "sneak around" in order to be together.

This led to numerous complications, as at least one, and probably two, of Peg's "best friends" were sharing our secret, but also were reporting back to Peg's mother. So Peg suggested we "cool it" until she got to college, when I would be able to meet her at the dorm, and we could date in reasonable privacy and peace. This only worked once until we found that the house mother at the dorm had been advised by Peg's parents, to not let me see her.

This was just too much and the next weekend Peg came home, she got hold of me through the grapevine, and we sneaked in a short date—which usually consisted of a walk around town, with a short stop for a few kisses at the center of the old covered bridge, and much conversation. On this date my personal dignity and been questioned, and my personal pride insulted. I felt I was as good a person as anyone and I did not feel very comfortable with things as they were. I could foresee no favorable outcome to the situation, so I made a proposal to Peg—not as an ultimatum (which of course it was) but rather as a counter attack. I said to Peg, "Honey, I love you and I know how much you love me; but I cannot, or will not, continue this sneaking around. Either you face up and tell your parents we are going together or we are going to have to run off and get married—even though we both know we are too young." (By now I was twenty; Peg was nineteen.)

Peg answered "No, I won't run off and get married. You're right—we are too young. And, as for telling my parents, well. Honey, that's impossible. You just don't know my father. You don't know his temper. It's just out of the question. I cannot do it."

There was quite a long pause now, as we walked along. We went several blocks, just walking arm in arm or holding hands quietly. As we got near enough to where Peg lived that we should not be seen together I spoke again. "Well then, I guess that's it. If you can't see me and you won't get married, well, I guess it's over—we'll have to break up. So! I give up. Your parents wanted to break us up and they have succeeded. I love you, but unless we can see each other openly or get married, it's over."

We stopped under a big maple tree, embraced, and kissed. Peg said with tear-moistened eyes, "Well then, I guess it's over, you've put me in a position where I have no choice." I said "Yes. And I guess I could say the same about you," and we parted.

I kept myself busy at the local pool hall in my off hours, or just sat around on that same park bench, where I had asked the "Spiritualist question."

Some of our mutual friends would come around, and a couple of Peg's "best friends" even tried to take advantage of my newly found "availability." I made up my mind that it was over and all the rules of love told me to circulate; friends told me, "There are lots of fish in the sea."

I remember on several occasions seeing Peg walking with her friends, on the way to a movie or something, and my heart jumped as I caught a glimpse of that long, flowing, satin blonde hair, bouncing off her shoulder as she walked; but I had to tell myself, "Forget it. It's all over."

Autumn was proceeding along, and I would always be at the high school football game on Friday night or Saturday, as the case my be, and it was just such an occasion when I noticed the back of that beautiful blonde head a few rows in front of me. Peg was home for the weekend and there she was, with two of her "best friends." Eventually she turned around and noticed me—maybe it was half time, I'm not sure—but we spoke to each other. The first time we had been close enough to each other to speak in maybe three or four months. Then Peg said, "Can I see you after the game? We're going to walk over to Wistie's house after the game. Could you walk along with us? I want to talk to you."

Well, walk we did and as soon as we arrived at Wistie's house, Jan and Wistie did a disappearing act like none Harry Houdini ever attempted. Peg and I were now alone together. Peg said, "My darling, I can't stand it like this, I just love you so much, I'll do anything. If you will still marry me, then I'll do it, as soon as you want to."

"Are you sure this is what you want?" I asked, knowing full well it was what I wanted. "Yes, Yes," she answered. "Just make arrangements and let's do it—let's get married."

Now I take the liberty to interject here, a little message to any of you over-protective, over-caring, over-possessive parents out there. Although I would not have had it any other way, I am sure that had Peg's parents been a little tolerant and allowed us to continue seeing each other, that we would have gone on, at least another year, maybe longer before marrying—if indeed we would have ended up marrying at all. The world of *what might have been* is a world full of hindsight and Monday morning quarter backing, and whatever you wish to imagine is *what might have been.*

Monday morning I immediately started making arrangements. I had heard that Cumberland, Maryland was a good "eloping place." After all, my brother "Bob" had eloped there about ten years ago.

So I bought tickets on the B&O RR to Cumberland, Maryland and we decided to do it early on Saturday morning, so Peg would not be missed until Monday morning if she signed out for the weekend "at home" and I would not miss too much work (since I really couldn't afford to lose any of my paycheck). I had accumulated about a hundred dollars—enough I thought, for the trip, and a day or two for our honeymoon.

So I got permission from my boss to take off a few days—whatever I needed, he said—just in case something unforeseen came up—and it did.

Saturday morning I was at the dorm, and Peg was ready to go. We each had a small overnight bag with the necessary essentials for a change of clothes, shaving, make-up etc.—and off we went, walking to the "B&O" station. What an exciting time. It was wonderful. We were both in ecstasy. I couldn't believe it; I had to pinch myself. There we were, not only back together again, but on our way to get married.

On the five-hour train ride, we talked excitedly about how and where to get married. I had heard somewhere that since Cumberland was a favorite elopement center, there were con artists around the courthouse who would, for a fee set up a wedding for you, provide transportation and so on, then charge an exorbitant sum of money. I would be on the alert for this—my Scotch blood would boil if I ever lost any of my meager funds to such a ruse.

Well surprise number one came when we applied for the marriage license and found that Maryland now had a three-day waiting period between the application and the granting of a license.

I said to Peg, "It's okay. We'll wait, we'll get a bus up to Johnstown. It's only a couple hours by bus and we can stay with my cousin Katherine while we wait it out."

We didn't know what the legal age was in Maryland and we didn't want to arouse any suspicions by asking, so we lied. I said I was twenty-two. Peg said she was twenty-one and that made us both legal. No proof was asked, and none given of course.

I guess the courthouse was open till noon on Saturdays and we arrived shortly before noon. We now had to wait until Tuesday for

37

our license, so we took a bus to Johnstown and "dropped in" on my cousin Katherine.

Katherine and her family had been renting my mother's house from her after I went into the Navy, since Mother had given up the house and gone to do live-in domestic work. When I first came out of the Navy, I had gone to live with Katherine for a few months before I went back to Ohio and Peggy. While I was living at Kay's home, she, having learned of my love affair with Peg, started a letter-writing friendship with Peg. So, although they had never met, they already were acquainted by mail and were quite good friends.

We were welcomed with joyously open arms on arrival at Kay's place. She assured us we were welcome to stay the two or three nights required for the waiting period. She had adequate sleeping space. Peg and I slept separately, of course, as none of us would ever have considered otherwise, until after the marriage. Funny how different we old fashioned folks were from the way people are today.

In the meantime, as according to Murphy's law, back at the dorm in Youngstown, for some reason—whether spontaneous or as a result of a call from the house mother—Peg's parents arrived at the dorm, and discovered Peg was missing. They searched her room and found one of the letters my cousin, Kay, had written to Peg. It revealed enough information to make her under suspicion of complicity. It took Peg's dad a day or two to assemble all the family and his attorney before heading for Katherine's house in Johnstown. Fortunately, he decided to first go to Altoona to pick up Peg's Aunt Mamie, who was the "old reliable" in anytime of need or trial and who could talk some sense into Peggy."

Well, the two little love bugs were blissfully unaware of all this and were impatiently awaiting the big day.

I called my brother Bob and told him what was going on, and he very graciously offered to take us to Cumberland in his car, where he and his wife would "stand up for us," or be witness to the marriage.

Early Tuesday morning Bob and Marion, his wife, came by to pick us up and off we went to Cumberland. We picked up our license at the courthouse, while Bob and Marion waited in the car a block or so down the street. Sure enough, as soon as we picked up our license, there suddenly appeared an older man, who, in a very kindly way, began to offer us the "package" wedding deal. Having been duly alerted to this scam I said to him, "Oh, no thanks. We're going to the First Presbyterian Church, where all the arrangements have been made." He said, "God bless you and good luck," and we went on our way, not knowing where we would go, but I had cleverly eluded the scam. And had unwittingly virtually saved our very skins.

As we crossed the street, and started toward where Bob had parked the car I saw a black Ford with an Ohio license plate, and said to Peg, "Hey, look." I think that's your father's car heading for the courthouse." She calmly said, "Oh, you're just paranoid; it couldn't possibly be." So we went back to the car and Bob drove around until we saw a church. It was a Lutheran church, so we knocked on the door of the parsonage, interrupting Dr. Sharpp's lunch, and proceeded to get married.

We didn't know until much later that, indeed, it had been Peg's family whom I had seen in the black Ford. They arrived at the courthouse five minutes after we had picked up our marriage license. The kindly old con man, who wasn't happy about missing out on a deal anyway, sent them on to the First Presbyterian Church. I've often wondered if he felt vindicated, thinking he had successfully saved an innocent maiden from the "lecherous lover."

Peg's father had arrived at Katherine's residence less than ten minutes after we had left there, so they were about that far behind us all the way from Johnstown to Cumberland—and we didn't know anything about it.

Katherine explained later that she had tried to divert them without really telling a lie, so she told them we were headed for some kind of New Cumberland or Cumberland or something like that in West Virginia or Kentucky—but she really wasn't sure. At any rate, if Peg's dad hadn't spent so much time trying to press Kay for information, and wanting her to tell him we had slept together (which we had not), he probably would have been able to catch up with us— perhaps at the very courthouse window—and Lord knows what that would have been like. But no matter. That also belongs in the world of *what might have been*.

When we arrived back in Johnstown, Bob dropped us off at the bus station. There would be a bus leaving for Youngstown, Ohio shortly. We decided to get back to Youngstown and back to the dorm, where Peg would sleep and we would delay making our next move—whatever that was going to be.

I would go on home to Newton Falls and come back to pick up Peg after I sorted things out. Well that changed very soon after our arrival at the dorm. I was waiting in the lobby, while Peg had gone upstairs to "check the waters." Suddenly Peg appeared from a fire exit door and said, "Lets get out of here fast. They've laid a trap for us, so lets go now." We hurried off—running down the street until we were far enough away from campus to feel a little secure. Then we went downtown to look for a hotel room. In 1947 you just didn't wander into a hotel at 10:00 P.M. without any luggage and ask for a room—especially if you looked like a couple of scared college kids. So, after being turned away at all the better hotels and spending another hour in doing so, it was now after 11:00 P.M. and we casually sauntered into one of the city's "less fashionable" flop houses— where you can rent "rooms by the hour" and succeeded in acquiring our "honeymoon suite." We figured we had better "consummate" our marriage in order to prevent any possibility of Peg's Dad having the marriage annulled, so we spent the night and half the next day attempting to accomplish that. We never really did get the job done, as it was on-the-job training for both of us; however, we *had* spent the night together, and for all purposes, that would suffice to convince people it was done.

The next day Peg decided to call her parents and let them know she was okay and that we were married. Little did she know about the drama that had just taken place, until she talked to her mother on the phone and found that we had been followed, or chased, to Cumberland.

That's when Peg had found out that the scheme was set up to "trap her" in the dorm when she came back! She was not to be allowed to leave, and was to face her parents there in the dorm; but some guardian angel had somehow left the stairwell access door unlocked that night and Peg had been able to get out by going down the rear stairway. Peg told me that she had never known of that door being left unlocked at night; but somehow on that night it was left unlocked and Peg was able to escape with her "Prince Charming."

After hanging up the phone, Peg told me that her mother insisted that she come home immediately to talk and Peg added that it was made plain that I was not invited to go along.

We discussed it a while and I said to Peg, "I'm your husband now; I don't want you to go there unless I go with you. We will face them together. But Peg said, "No, that won't work." I began to feel as though Peg was feeling like backing out, so I said to her, "You do what you really want to do. If you think that's what you want, then, go ahead, go home to your parents."—and she did just that!

Next day I went to see a lawyer—only because some of the friends around town told me that Peg's Dad was going to annul the marriage and have me arrested for kidnapping under the "Mann Act."

The lawyer assured me that none of this could happen to me. It may be possible to annul the marriage—but not unless Peg agreed to it, because she was over eighteen years of age.

I heard nothing more from Peg for two days, and I assumed that now it really was all over for us. I was literally "going through hell." Peg had forsaken me and gone back to the family she had deserted. *Oh well, I'll survive, I thought, Nothing ever works out right for me.* I didn't have much self esteem anyway, so what was new.

With Peg back home, and me not knowing what to do, I went back to work, to face all my co-workers and my boss, who had taken a collection and bought us a nice wedding gift and who were all anxious to hear about the wedding and honeymoon. How could I tell them that Peg had gone back home—and that I didn't know what the outcome was to be? So I didn't tell them.

After work, as was my usual custom, I stopped in at my very good friend "Mom" Taylor's house.

Mom Taylor was the most adorable, loveable, Christian person I had ever met and the Taylor home was always a good place to get a home-cooked supper. On this day, as I entered Mom Taylor's house, she had an unusually sly almost cat-like expression and with a grin she said, "Wally, I want you to look in my bedroom."

There reclining on the bed was my very own bride, wallowing in the largest pile of dimes I had ever seen.

Peg had stood her ground. She told her parents her choice was made and that if it had to be a choice between family and Wally it was going to be Wally.

So her dad disowned her—invited her to leave and not darken his door again. And her mother—well, she gave Peggy her savings bank full of dimes—almost four hundred dollars in dimes—kissed her and said, "Good luck my little darling. I'll always be in touch, I'll always be here if you need me." Peggy knew where to go, to Mom Taylor's house, where she waited for Prince Charming to come home from work.

CHAPTER XI
MARRIED LIFE—THE EARLY YEARS

The first few years were really rough. Peg's Father had disowned her for running off with such an uneducated low brow from the hills of Pennsylvania. Jobs were tough to find and even one room to live in was almost impossible to find. The post-war weddings and baby boom were in full swing. Cars and living quarters were on hold at pre-war status, so scarce was the watch word.

We decided to move to Prescott, Arizona, where my sister was now living and owned a few small rental units on their property, one of which was available. We asked her to hold it and packed and shipped all our worldly goods to Prescott.

We planned to go to Johnstown first for a visit with Mother (no longer "Mama") and Bradley. Bradley was an old family friend, and relative by marriage, since his brother Elton was married to my Uncle Ed's daughter. Mother was working as a housekeeper for Bradley, and as it turned out, since her baby was now grown and married, she and Bradley decided to marry. I wish I had time and space to expound on this union, it lasted seventeen years till Bradley died in Yuma, Arizona, where they had lived for nine of the seventeen years.

All I can say is that no finer man ever lived, than Bradley Straw. The whole family loved this wonderful, quiet man, who worked as a car inspector on the Cambria and Indiana Railroad. Black lung from the coal caused his early disability retirement to Arizona, and ultimately, his death in 1965. Many friends and family members commented that Edna had been able to marry the two finest men that God ever created. I knew Bradley. He and I were like father and son, and like brothers, at the same time. My own father would have been proud to endorse him as the man to fill the void in my life. I cannot say enough about this good, good man.

But my digression has been too lengthy. We're still moving to Prescott, Arizona, and visiting Mother and Bradley in Nanty Glo, Pennsylvania. Our tickets were reserved on the El Capitan to Flagstaff—or maybe it was the Chief—one or the other. But when Peggy and Mother got together, the plans were changed and we were now moving back to Johnstown so I could enroll in the Veterans' High School Program through the G.I. Bill of Rights and get my high school diploma.

All our belongings were shipped back from Arizona, I graduated in September 1948, just one month after the birth of our first child—a petite red head we named Diane Grace.

Not quite a year later, I was laid off from my job in a machine shop and we returned to Warren, Ohio where I procured employment by the company with whom I would stay until I would retire after nearly thirty-five years of service in September of 1982. Thanks to the high school diploma, I was able to get the position of machinist apprentice in the tool and die shop of the Niles, Ohio stamping plant, which began my career.

When Grandpa Bailey heard rumors that he had a granddaughter and that we might be living back in Warren, Ohio, it was just too much for him to endure, and we were invited back into his good grace. Speaking of Graces, his wife never did let Peg out of her contact, and often sneaked visits and financial help to her "darlings." No more fitting name was ever bestowed on a person than that of Grace Peoples Bailey. She was full of grace.

CHAPTER XII
THE CAREER BEGINS

When I was laid off from the machine shop in Johnstown, I decided to take the week of vacation I had coming and take a trip back to Warren, Ohio, where, I thought, job hunting would be more fruitful.

I found it not much better than Johnstown. One day while applying at the State of Ohio Employment Services office in Warren, and after having been told there was nothing out there, I said to the agent, "Look, is there any place that will let me work for them for free until I'm able to learn enough to prove my worth and get paid?" He explained that such a thing was against the law, even if anyone might be agreeable.

As I thanked him and started to walk out, he said, "Hey, wait a minute. Come back here." He was reaching into his desk, while continuing to talk and he pulled out a postcard-sized piece of paper. "Here," he said, "you might try this. There is a plant in Niles called The Niles Steel Products Company and they are looking for applicants with high school diplomas who can pass some stiff entrance tests, to become machinist apprentices."

"Sure," I said, "I'll try anything."

At the Niles Steel Products Company I was introduced to Mr. F. A. Snow, the plant industrial engineer, who was also training supervisor.

Al, as Mr. Snow was called, explained that I would need to be pretty good in algebra, geometry, and some principles of physics, and would have to endure an eight-hour bank of tests—including academic and personality characteristics and so on. In addition to that, I would have to write three 500 word essays on subjects which would be furnished to me. Al made it all sound pretty tough—and it was—but, being desperate, I was game.

It was all set, and Mr. Snow was to notify me by mail of the date of the examination. I had to have my essays with me when I reported for the tests.

Back home in Johnstown, we began making preparations to move to Warren. Movers required three to four weeks notice. The date was set and the truck was to pick up our furniture on June twelfth, and deliver it to our apartment in Warren, on June thirteenth.

While we prepared and waited for the movers, the letter came from Al Snow, "Please report at 8:00 A.M. on Tuesday, June fourteenth for apprenticeship examinations."

The truck came for the furniture, and as luck would have it, some old friends of my mother's from Belsano, Pennsylvania, who now lived in Warren, Ohio, were visiting the area and would be travelling home to Warren on June twelfth. They very graciously offered to give Peg and me a ride to Warren with them. We stayed overnight with the friends, and when they delivered us to our Federal Housing Authority concrete-slab apartment, the furniture was already there. The apartment was a dirty, greasy, filthy mess and our furniture and belongings all lay in a pile in the so called living room.

After we bought a few groceries and eked out a lunch, Peg reminded me that tomorrow morning was the testing and I had better get ready.

I had not written the essays yet, I couldn't remember the titles, and I couldn't find the letter among the jumble of furniture and "stuff." *What shall I do?* I wondered. I couldn't even find writing paper, pen and ink. (The essays had to be written with a nib pen, you know, the old school pen you dip in the inkwell.)

I said to Peg, "Forget it, there's no way I'll ever make it." She then uttered the most profound statement I had ever heard anyone utter. "You're right," she said, "There is no way you are going to make it—*if you don't try.* But, if you think hard, you can remember the essay titles, and I'm sure they sell paper and pens and ink down at the corner store. If you try, you might have a chance. If you give up, you don't have any chance at all."

Faced with the challenge, I did, indeed, remember the titles, buy the writing materials, write the essays and—by the skin of my teeth—passed the tests, along with one other successful candidate. Ten more unfortunate fellows did not succeed.

It took three long weeks before I was advised of the test results and another month before I was called to work, but it all paid off. My little bride had inveigled me into getting the diploma and shamed me into going through with the tests.

My one regret is that I never got back to the employment office to let the nice gentleman know I had succeeded. Thanks to his last-second afterthought. I hope he found out, so he could feel good about it too.

I decided to work this chapter in for two reasons—one, so you could learn of Peg's profound support—the other so I could reveal the following dream.

After about three years of apprenticeship under my belt, and one to go, I had a strange dream. In the dream a big shot from the office came down into the shop looking for me. He took me and the shop general foreman into the general foreman's office, and together they informed me I was to be made foreman soon, and that my starting salary would be $452.00 per month.

Well that was quite a dream, since I was then making about half that, and as for needing a foreman, they were far from that.

Six months after completing the apprenticeship, as I was working the afternoon shift, I noticed the works manager come into the shop and speak to the foreman. It was about 5:30 or 5:45 P.M. To see the works manager in the machine shop was a rare sight prior to five in the evening—let alone after that. Something was up and I sensed it. I then noticed they both looked my way and the foreman pointed toward me.

The works manager came over, introduced himself and invited me to go into the general foreman's office with him, where we could "talk."

We just chatted; he asked some pointed questions, but nothing really happened that day. But I knew something was up.

Ultimately I learned the corporation had decided to select several apprentice graduates—one from my division, which had about a half dozen candidates, and two others from the other corporate divisions—to be trained as industrial engineers in a pilot program to see how the corporation's apprenticeship graduates would stack up against college graduates.

Yes. I was the lucky fellow who was chosen from our division and when I was called up to the work manager's office to be asked if I would accept the position, I was told my starting salary would be $452.00 per month! After three years of industrial and mechanical engineering training I was made general foreman of maintenance, and although some changes had resulted in the closing down of the tool and die shop, I was now the boss—and I think my dream was pretty darned close to accurate.

CHAPTER XIII
MY FIRST EXPERIENCE AT LILY-DALE

We had no automobile and I had no driver's license, but public transportation was abundant and we got by fine. On frequent weekends we were invited on trips with Peg's family to various places.

One such trip was about a three-hour drive to western New York State, to visit an old family friend named Hilda Wolff who, as it turned out, just happened to live in Lily-Dale, New York, a private summer camp of the, yes you guessed it, the Spiritualist Church. I felt like a heretic—dirty and evil. *What am I doing here? What have I got myself into?* I thought to myself, *Peg really is a Spiritualist and I married her anyway! Well, What God hath put together let no man put asunder*—and besides, I had taken a solemn vow with my bride. I would never forsake such a commitment. Our love for each other was true, I would just see this thing through. I would check it out, prove it's a bunch of hooey, and bring my family to the Lord my way.

The camp had various offerings, one of which was called a message service, where several mediums would take turns at the podium, delivering messages from spirit loved ones, to members of the congregation.

At one such of these services, on a rainy Saturday afternoon, the people gathered.

There were no mediums present to conduct the program. None of the scheduled "workers" had even shown up, so the program director recruited reluctant volunteers from among those present.

An elderly man named Gomer Davis, who was the gate keeper at the main entrance to the camp, was persuaded to come up front and work. Peggy and I were seated toward the rear. Suddenly, Gomer called out loudly, "Walter! Is there a Walter here?"

Three of us raised our hands. Gomer then said, "Well, I have a spirit here named Walter, who wants to talk to a Walter in the audience." One of the other two Walters dropped his hand, but two of us were still hanging in there.

Then Gomer said, "Wait a minute. This Walter says his name is Albert, but that they called him Walter." The other Walter now dropped his hand—and I almost dropped. Who could have known this? Who could have told him? Peggy didn't even know this at that time, so her father could not have known, so nobody was cheating.

My thoughts were too overwhelming to comprehend. Gomer continued. He pointed to me and said, "Yes, you are the one. This is your father. He says he passed over in a railroad accident." I answered, "Yes." I don't remember anything else Gomer said that day—nor anything else that happened that weekend, but I knew one thing for sure—this stuff was real—and if it was of the devil I was in big trouble, because now I had gone and rousted my dad out of heaven and dragged him into this silly place.

But how could my father be in heaven and be a demon? Oh, that's right—demons will impersonate anyone, even Jesus, when they can get away with it. I told Peg, "I'm never coming back to this place again and we are joining a church and getting straight so we can raise our daughter properly."

Peg said, "Okay, whatever you wish, but you can't change what is."

In the passing years I have come to grips with the dilemma and will, later on in this book, explain my resolution to the question. But, at that time, we did get back into church. I did not stop going on the occasional weekend trips to Lily-Dale and slowly became more comfortable with it, and more open to it—eventually having private "readings" myself—one of which I will delve into in some detail as we move along.

I can't tell you the extent to which Gomer Davis' messages had stimulated my curiosity, but my engineering outlook on life urged me to find out more of this—find some clue as to the real source of Gomer's information.

Peg's father was very learned in parapsychology, had one of the finest personal libraries on the subject in existence, and was a voracious reader. I was still stinging from the afterglow of his attitude about me and my marriage to his daughter, so it was very difficult for me to warm to this man for many years. We were 180 degrees apart on virtually every aspect of life. He was a devoted "New Deal" democrat with personal acquaintances the like of Harry Hopkins and owned numerous letters from President Roosevelt, with photos etc. But to me, he was a "liberal" who espoused the Townsend Plan, which, to my training, was certain economic poison. On religion, you have read my background. His was almost agnostic, except that his Masonic beliefs in a divine creator kept him searching. He just couldn't accept the deity of Jesus Christ. He considered him merely a great man and one of the world's great teachers, or masters.

So there was not much common ground, but he was my father-in-law and—whether family, friend, or enemy—I'm supposed to love him. So we began to relate. I began to understand something about Dana M. Bailey Jr.

He was not a Spiritualist, but considered himself a "scientific investigator" in the area of psychic phenomena. I could buy into that. I'm an engineer, not by college degree, but by profession and the school of hard knocks. So I could espouse that idea. Maybe I could learn from him and look further into this "psychic phenomena."

The next jolt came when Peg and I were driving towards home from a weekend at Hilda's in Lily-Dale. (We now had our own car and I had my driver's license. We'll talk about that later too.)

Peg was telling me that she would like to stop in Westfield, New York on the way home and get a reading from "Madam Christina."

This was new to me. "Who is Madam Christina?" I asked. "Well, she's just a nice lady who lives in an old mansion a few blocks up the street from the Welsh Grape Juice Company offices." She boards elderly poor folks and gives psychic readings, but has no rapport with Spiritualists or with Lily-Dale, only twenty miles away.

I agreed to stop and said I would wait in the car while Peg went inside for a reading.

After the reading, while motoring homeward to Warren, Ohio, we discussed the reading. Madam Christina had asked Peg if there was a "John" on her husband's side of the family. She thought this "John" had already passed on because she saw the symbolism of either burning flames or running water, as in a stream. (I can see the similarity—when I mentally picture a running stream, reflecting the sunlight, I see that it could also look like flames.) Anyway, Christina said that he either had passed, or would pass, from this life by fire or by drowning.

Having never known my grandfather, Edna's father, I did not know that his name was John Davis, nor do I know to this day how he may have died.

The only John I knew was the youngest son of my oldest brother, whom they called "Jackie," and who was a baby, only about a year old—the same age as our own daughter, Diane. This bothered me. Was this really going to happen? Should I warn Bob, so he could watch out for this?

I finally decided this whole business was too "kooky" and I would do nothing but upset my brother, and maybe even cause a family rift and it wasn't worth it—over such nonsense as this—so I kept my mouth closed on the matter.

On that fateful day, about a year and a half after Christina had mentioned the "John" message, I received a telegram over the telephone, informing me of the death of little Jackie.

There was a mix-up in the telegram wording and a written copy was never sent to me. The result was that I missed the funeral service, much to my enduring regret.

Jackie had wandered off while playing, had fallen into a little stream nearby, and drowned.

So this was John and it was rippling water, not flames, that Christina had seen in her revelation.

I'm not sure whether I ever have mentioned any of this to my brother, so if and when he reads this, it may well be his first knowledge of this strange event. It's not something that would be easy to talk about.

CHAPTER XIV
MY PSYCHIC PROBLEM SOLVER

I was not planning to talk about work accomplishments, as they tend to be technical and boring to many folks, and smack of self aggrandizement to all; but I have decided to interject just a few examples of challenges that bore outstanding results.

Now that the stamping plant and tool and die shop was relocated to Cleveland, the major product of our division became confined to steel shipping containers such as pails, drums, buckets and fifty-five gallon steel drums most people call barrels.

The federal government had placed an order with us for hundreds of thousands of containers, which we came to call water cans.

They were to be placed in fallout shelters, filled with fresh drinking water and used in the event of a nuclear attack. The water cans had a polyethylene liner, and when empty were to be used as sanitary stations—yes, that's right.

The government specs mandated that these containers be made from lighter gage material than we had ever used before, so some definite engineering problems were to be faced. The cans were to hold twenty gallons with one percent error factor, with a friction lid that could be readily installed and removed, yet would not fall off when the can was turned upside down.

The steel from which the cans were to be made was ordered, and was painted, lacquered and lithographed in the flat. Over one hundred new employees were hired to staff the assembly line for three shifts, seven days a week; but the engineering problems continued. The lids would not stay on, the double seam that sealed the bottom to the can leaked, and the cans buckled on the sides when put in the flanging machine.

We paid the workers to wipe the steel sheets with clean cloths, wearing clean gloves, while efforts were made to correct the problems. Time was passing, money was flowing out, and we could not ship one can. The contract had a penalty clause in it, which meant that if we didn't meet our shipping schedules, we paid the government. The first penalty of $60,000 was fast approaching.

I kept insisting to my immediate boss that I knew how to solve the problems, but he was an expert on containers, a graduate mechanical engineer, and he had no patience with me. Finally he said, "Walter, you go up to the other plant and stay out of here and leave me alone."

I became depressed and discouraged and retired to my desk in the pool area of the main office, just outside the division manager's office. There I lamented my case and talked with the now-idle government inspectors, who had to approve the cans before shipping. The two inspectors had empathy for our situation, as well as for the position in which I now found myself.

The division manager, Vic, had just recently been promoted from the position of division chief industrial engineer to that of division manager.

He was the finest, nicest, "straightest shooter" I had ever met in the company. I almost thought of him as an uncle.

After about another week of frustration and no progress in solving the problems, I got up my nerve. I walked in Vic's office and asked permission to speak with him.

Upon approval I began, "Vic, would you be willing to listen to some of my suggestions on the water can problems?" He replied, "Walter, I'm at my wits end. I'm willing to listen to anybody who can make some sense out of this mess. We are going down the tube fast."

"Well, I must first tell you I have been trying to make these suggestions to Mr. _____, but he is not interested and has told me to stay out of the plant. Vic, I don't like going over my boss' head, but this is urgent."

I went on, "If I draw three sketches for you, that spell out the problems and solutions, and they make sense to you, will you let me do the things I propose?"

"I'm listening," he replied.

He studied my sketches, listened to my proposals and said, "Well by God it makes sense to me Walter. How long will it take to make these modifications?"

I answered, "If you let me have the dies today, I'll get them to my machine shop up at the other plant, and we should be ready for production Monday morning on the day shift."

"Well," Vic said, "You aren't really going over anybody's head. Mr. _____'s office is in Youngstown and you are in charge here anyway. Let's take a walk."

We walked together down to the plant, where Mr. _____ was with the die setter and a young engineer at the lid stamping press.

"How's it going?" asked Vic. Mr. _____ looked up, and I'm sure, suspected something when he saw me, whom he had ordered out of the plant. "Oh, not so good, Vic. Still can't get these damned lids to stay on."

Vic spoke, "Well, why don't you go ahead back to your office in Youngstown, because Walter and I are going to try some things for a few days. I'll get back to you when I need you."

By Monday morning the three machines in question were set up. The flanger, the double seamer, and the lid presses. The line started up and the inspectors stepped in. The first can was good and so were the next 200,000 or so.

We did not have to pay the $60,000 penalty and we still made a small profit on the total order.

Something told me to do it.

The second event occurred after Mr. _____ and I had made unspoken amends and were now back in sync again. He is a super engineer, a great guy and as bull headed as any Dutchman ever was, but over all we were good friends and still are.

Anyway Mr. _____ challenged me to design a "barrel head" die that would produce a fully formed barrel head in one hit of the press and have a "pre-curl" feature—a radius on the edge of the flange.

Well this was a challenge, since accomplished engineers in the steel drum industry had never been able to come up with such a design. But "something told me" I could do it. So during the ten weeks of the steel strike in 1959, I, being in management, worked on this die design and felt I had gotten it. Mr. _____ looked it over, said, "Walt, I think it will work."

The drawings were sent out to vendors for quotations. One of the most prestigious equipment manufacturers and designers of steel container equipment in the world, located in northern California, responded: "We will build the dies to your specifications for $25,000 each. But we must inform you we take no responsibility for their success, it is our opinion that they will not work."

Several others came in with lower bids, and no such comments; however we felt all bids were too high. I entered a proposal that we build them in my shop for $10,000 each. We did just that and they worked beautifully. We built a spare die, and word got around about our "barrel head" line. *Iron Age* magazine requested permission to come in and do a complete article, with photographs, on the line.

The general manager would not permit it. Nobody was going to see our secret.

Those dies are still pounding away at the steel container plant in Nitro, West Virginia, over thirty years later.

One more and I'll quit blowing my horn. With two "barrel plants" gong—one in Niles and now the new one in Nitro, West Virginia—we went through many sheets of steel in a day. Our new automatic welding machine had a serious problem, with a part of the feeder mechanism that was built by that same company in California.

Each sheet (approximately six feet long and three feet wide) had to be shot-blasted on both edges, top and bottom, to prepare the steel for the welding that would turn the sheet into a cylinder, which would become a barrel.

There was a problem with "out of square" sheets which we could not overcome, so an excessive number of sheets were not being shot-blasted accurately on the edge, and thus, would not weld properly. This resulted in a scrap sheet and wasted production time.

"Something told me" that if we mounted one pair of shot-blast nozzles in a spring-loaded set of guide rollers, the problem would be solved.

I said nothing, just went to the drawing board and drew it up. After I was satisfied it would work, I presented it to Mr. _____, and together we presented it to the general manager.

The go-ahead was given. One unit was built and installed at Niles. It worked so well that scrap was virtually eliminated and another unit was built for installation at the Nitro plant.

The first-year savings in scrap alone was over $200,000 at each plant, and as far as I know, those dies are still operating today, although the Niles plant has long since been sold to another container company.

If I had never done another thing during my almost thirty-five years with the corporation, I would still have contributed, in hard cash returns, enough savings that all of the monies they ever paid me during those thirty-five years—including my benefits, and pension payoff—would not have amounted to half of one percent of the total savings.

And yet I can still hear the raspy snarling voice of that nincompoop who was eventually to become general superintendent of maintenance services when he asked me, shortly before my premature retirement, "What have you done for me lately?"

No matter—he wasn't bright enough to know anyway. That is part of the reason I express resentment, and refuse to name the corporation. For there were to be many, many more similar accomplishments through the years. Those were just a few, but I feel they well represent my worth to my corporation.

One post script: years after having been transferred up the ladder, back to Industrial Engineering again, I noticed the name tag on the security guard a the main gate, one day as I was entering the plant. "John Edmundson. Are you Vic Edmundson's son?" I queried.

"Yes I am—and who are you?" "I'm Walter Cameron. I once worked for your Dad."

He smiled a wide grin, now looking exactly like his father, came over to the car window, extended his right hand and said, "So, you are Walter Cameron? I've heard Dad talk about you and what you did for him, and believe me, Walter, he will always be grateful for what you did and will never forget you. I'm pleased to meet you— and 'thanks' from me too."

Enough said. That was worth more than money could buy, but it still doesn't buy groceries.

Since I am moralizing, I'll try your patience once again to demonstrate some of my attitudes, and my own *naivete*.

I always believed that a dedicated effort and a loyal heart were the keys to success; so I lived and worked accordingly and presumed that any merited rewards, as a result, just automatically would come to pass.

I had never reckoned with intrigue or subterfuge—it was never a part of my id—and I always thought a friend was a friend.

This is just to be one example of a lesson, hard learned but never heeded, as I always have, and always will, honor a friendship with truth and loyalty, in spite of such things as that which I am about to relate.

Following the training program, of which I was one of the "pilot" members, there came a subsequent group of trainees. These seemed to me to be more aggressive and ruthless in their character.

They did all the right things—they played golf and poker, and drank and cursed a lot, and seemed to much more interested in "show boating" than they were in making a profit for the company.

They did (on the positive side) attend night school at Youngstown State University or other nearby colleges and obtain degrees—which I did not. I had the responsibility of a family, and a job that often demanded my time at any hour of the day or night. So along with my lack of self-confidence and my skimpy high school background, I felt I could not do that. So I never obtained a degree.

One of these trainees became a rather close friend of mine (I thought); we were "Brother Masons" and we both had an over-compelling addiction to the high school football and basketball teams in Warren. We frequently attended out-of-town games together and rarely if ever missed any game. (This was so well known about me, that occasionally I would be paged on the PA system at a game and told to report to the plant for an "emergency.")

Warren had a pretty good basketball team that particular year, so all the games took on an added importance, since we expected the team to advance well in the state tournament.

On this particular instance, I had been ill with a rather miserable cold or flu, had been ill almost a week, and had missed work Tuesday and Wednesday as a result. I had gone to work on Monday, as sick as a dog, but knowing my position of responsibility, I had to be there, on Monday especially.

On Thursday I returned to work, feeling a little better, but still really so sick that I should not have been at work. I began to feel somewhat better as the day went on, and about mid-day I received a telephone call from my "friend" whom I have just described to you.

Our beloved Warren Panthers (now called the Raiders) were to play a very tough game in the Akron area that night and I had resigned myself to listening to the radio broadcast of the game. My office phone rang and it was my "friend." "Hey, Walter, let's go to the game tonight—I'll drive."

I replied, "No thanks." I've been off sick several days, and still have a bad cold, and in this weather (about nine inches of snow on the ground and temperature in the 'zero' area), I could not possibly go.

He coaxed, "I told you I'll drive." I replied, "No. Your car is a rag top anyway, and it would be too cold." "Come on, Walter." he coaxed. "I'll let you sit right next to the heater so you can stay warm and I promise to drop you off right at the entrance before I park my car, so you won't even need to walk in the cold weather."

He coaxed and coaxed and finally I stupidly relented and took him up on his promise.

He picked me up at home and had with him another mutual acquaintance, was a classmate of mine while "going through the degrees" in masonic work.

The friend sat in the rear, and as promised, I sat in front next to the heater.

I had dosed up on cold medicine, and felt pretty good—until we arrived at the fieldhouse, where the game was to be played, where, instead of dropping me off at the door, my "friend" proceeded to park—about a quarter of a mile from the fieldhouse. This cold walk caused me to begin a relapse, and by the time the game was over (we lost), the walk back to the car was torture and I was really getting sick.

"Let's get in that car and get the heat going," I said. And get me home."

Well now came the big surprise—the driver now said, "Oh, didn't I tell you? I have a friend here in this town who owns a tavern, and I promised him I would stop in after the game." My objections were overruled with, "We'll just stay long enough for one drink—after all, a good shot of whiskey will help your cold."

Well, I was not a social drinker at this time in my life—in fact I was a teetotaler, but the sound of a warming, medicinal shot made some sense, so we went to the tavern.

The friends all began visiting among themselves, and after introductions, I had "one" shot and begged their indulgence in my non-social behavior. I laid my head down one the bar and tried to be comfortable and time passed, and passed, and passed.

I kept nagging my "friend," "Please, let's go home. I'm sick." But he tossed aside all my pleading and went on enjoying himself, as he was wont to do.

Finally, closing time came (2:30 A.M.) and we left. I had no drinks, other than the one medicinal shot of whiskey.

Arriving at my home at about 4:00 A.M. and feeling half dead, I fell into bed and into a deep sleep. I didn't awaken until almost 1:00 P.M. My loving wife never attempted to waken me, as she knew I was not well, but she also never thought to call in and report me off work. So I missed Friday, another very important day, as it was necessary for me to line up all the weekend maintenance and repair work.

My "friend," who was a "macho" man of iron, was able to get to work as usual on Friday, even after having been up half of the night—or rather all night.

On Monday I was well enough to return to work properly, and with much chagrin and worry over not having been "reported off," I was asked quite a few times, "where the hell were you Friday?"—as I had expected.

But the big blow came when I got a telephone call from Vic Edmundson, now the division manager, calling me to his office.

Immediately as I entered his office he asked me, "Where were you Friday, Walter?" I answered, "I was sick—very sick. My wife never awakened me, I was so sick. You knew I was off work Tuesday and Wednesday didn't you?" I asked.

Yes, he knew that, but he went on. "Mr. Bruhn (the manufacturing vice president) had been in for a meeting Friday, and your name came up. He wanted to ask you some questions and we couldn't locate you. We found out that you were absent, and wondered why, when this guy"—(he gestured toward the adjacent office of my "friend" who was out of his office at the moment, and had recently replaced Vic as divisional industrial engineer) "This guy," he went on, "said, 'Well, I don't know why Walter isn't here, I was out drinking with him most of the night last night, and I'm here!'"

Now, I tell you, that is an example of the character of the people my company selected to fill their top management positions. I could never figure out how Vic had achieved the manager's position—he was such a straight shooter. I went on to explain the whole story exactly s it happened—and admitted it was a stupid thing to do—but I certainly didn't expect that kind of a low blow from Mr. "Hot Shot."

Mr. Hot Shot went on to one more upper management position before leaving the corporation. Fortunately, he had an impressive resume and was able to keep on finding good jobs—about once a year for several years.

And as for "Vic," he was just too honest and straight shooting, so the underminer's eventually got him and he was relegated to finishing his career polishing the seat of his blue serge trousers in the industrial engineering headquarters office.

CHAPTER XV
THE DRIVER'S EXAM

I promised to tell you about my driver's license. I'll try to keep it brief.

Peg's dad had spent two hundred dollars on a 1937 Pontiac two-door sedan, which he gave to me so we could have transportation. Also—by "coincidence"—Peg's dad and mother were planning an extended six-week motoring tour of Mexico and the Southwest United States in a month or so, and they had asked me if we would mind staying at their house in Newton Falls, while they were on this tour. Mr. Bailey had a small furniture business which he operated out of the large old house. We were to "mind the store" and I could drive the fifteen miles each way to my job in Niles, Ohio. Thus the car—and thus the need to get a driver's license.

I did a lot of practice driving and already knew the basics, having done a little before. But one of the requirements of the test was that you parallel park your car between two flags, and six inches from an old telephone pole that simulated a street side curb.

This was set up in a crescent-shaped gravel parking lot—with no street, or anything else to help you get aligned. I was the last of about eight or ten examinees, some of whom passed, some of whom failed.

My turn came and one thing I had neglected to do was to practice parallel parking. I have never even attempted to park a car before; but I had studied the book, and knew the theory of when and how much to turn the steering wheel, and so on, in order to park.

I had heard that you get three chances to park before you are failed. At least, I hoped this was true, because on my first attempt I was backed up at a right angle to the make-believe curb. The trooper said, "Pull out and try again." The second attempt was better. I was now parked parallel to the curb, between the standards—and a full four feet away from the curb. The trooper came over to my car window and inquired, "Have you ever parked a car before?"

"Well," he said sternly, "pull up and try it one more time, but this will have to be your last chance—and remember—don't bump the standard."

So I pulled out again, and pulled the car into the prescribed pre-parking position. This old Pontiac had such high windows that you could not possibly see anything below the level of a parking meter head and the rear windows were two small holes near the roof, pointed almost skyward, so that to see what I was about to do was out of the question.

I hesitated, placed both hands on the steering wheel, then laid my head down on the steering wheel and prayed, "Lord, Dear Lord, you know I can't park this car, and I know I can't park this car, so Lord—you are going to have to park it for me. Please, Lord, park this car for me. Amen."

I raised my head—never opened my eyes—I just put her in reverse and turned the wheel the prescribed number of times in the prescribed manner, and stopped the car.

The trooper came over, opened the car door and said, "That's fine. Now lets go for a ride, and for God's sake, don't bump that standard while you are pulling out."

God had parked that car perfectly and I got my driver's license and you can laugh all the way to the insane asylum if you wish, but that is exactly what happened. God and I know that.

CHAPTER XVI
THE READING

During the late winter months in early 1956, Peg and I, along with Diane, who was now nearly eight years of age, made a weekend trip to Lily-Dale to visit Hilda Wolff.

The camp is closed in the winter, but many of the residents stay year round. Hilda worked part time at the Lily-Dale post office and during the camping "season" she rented sleeping rooms to camp visitors, as her means of support.

Lily-Dale is a beautiful place at any time, but even more so in the winter. Hilda lived a lonesome life, so we enjoyed visiting with her.

As I said, the camp was closed, but this weekend I had decided to stop at madam Christina's place for a reading on the way home on Sunday afternoon.

I had not yet met Christina, so we thought it best if Peg stayed out of sight, in the car, so there would be no chance for Christina to have any advance knowledge of who I was. As I entered and was being greeted by Christina, I was also analyzing her from every standpoint I could, in those brief moments. She was obviously in her late fifties or early sixties, I thought, and she had a reddish tint to her hair that most likely was an add-on feature. She had the strangest eyes I have ever seen, a mystic pale blue, almost azure blue, and as big as saucers—I guess "pop-eyed" is the best description—and from the side, I could see a transparent thickness or lens on her eyes that seemed to be almost a quarter of an inch thick. I had only ever seen this phenomenon once before, on a woman I had seen in the Pennsylvania Railroad Depot in Pittsburgh. This passing glimpse of a stranger in Pittsburgh had stuck with me, and as I gazed at Christina, I remembered that woman.

I wondered if they had a similar ailment of the eyes. It never occurred to me then that it possibly could have been the same woman I was now facing. I'll never know that.

Christina was very cordial, and we just chit-chatted about the weather. She wanted to know if I had ever had a reading before. She seemed ready to spend all the time either of us cared to that afternoon.

She began with a prayer, and informed me that she was a Catholic. But she assured me that would make no difference, since what I was about to hear was a revelation from God and God doesn't care about sect or denomination.

She asked me if I preferred tarot cards, tea leaves, or astrology, or none of the above. I chose none of the above and told her I wasn't comfortable with any of those. "Fine," she said, "I don't really use them anyway. They are just props I use to accommodate people's preference."

She said, "I don't claim that what I get comes from spirits, or departed relatives but, however it comes, it comes from God."

We were now ready to begin. I don't know where to begin, so I'll list as many items as I can recall, then follow that with what I believe to be the outcome, or fulfillment of the same.

"You are married, and I have read for your wife before. Why do I see two children? Do you have two children?"

"No, we have only one child, a girl," I said.

Christina said, "You are going to have another. Your wife is pregnant now."

"Oh! I didn't know that—but if you say so—we'll see."

"It will be a boy and—I don't wish to alarm you but—I see a problem. He may be stillborn or, if not, there is a problem—a darkness—about the head, with this child." She went on, "You know, when we see things like this, they can be changed with prayer. So you will need to pray over this child... You will have another child as well, much later, and that too will be a boy and this one will be a very special child. He will be a real chip off the old block—and I don't mean you," she said with a long smile.

"He will love things that move, I mean like, trains, and busses and things that go up and down, like airplanes. In fact, he will choose one of these as his life's work—although he could be a brain surgeon," she said almost as an after thought.

I didn't realize her meaning and took it literally—that he would become a brain surgeon, when all she really meant was that he *could* if he so desired. He would have the capability to do so.

Christina continued, "This will be the most difficult of all your children to raise, but you will succeed and he will also be the greatest gratification to you in his adult life."

She went on to explain in detail the various positions I would hold, and the location of my jobs, all with the same company but in three different cities, which she generally identified. All of these things came to pass with uncanny accuracy.

Then she said, You have a brother who has been in Africa—perhaps during the war? I said, "Yes."

"Well, he's going back again, more or less to fill his need to turn his swords into plowshares if you know what I mean. This time he will teach. I see some sort of, not exactly missionary work, but similar, but more of a teaching thing—and this time—he will not return. He will stay there. But again I must say, this too can be changed with prayer."

Now Christina looked at me and said, "You too are going to cross the water, you are going to cross the water not once, but twice—and it will be on business. The company you work for will send you."

Now, I knew this was ridiculous—me, a tool-and-die maker machinist, turned industrial engineer. I was just a trainee and my company had no interest overseas. (I would like to digress and interject here that my long-standing resentment toward my company for never having duly recognized my great contributions and accomplishments to their benefit, causes me to reciprocate by not naming the company, thus depriving them of any recognition from me.)

Now the subject turned to domestic matters. "You will sell the house you now live in." *Big deal*, I thought. *What else am I going to do—burn it down?*

"You will buy a newer, more modern home—not a new home—but a newer home. This will be a brick house. It will not be in the city, but rather in a township just a few hundred feet outside the city limits. This will look like a ranch house from the road as if it has only one floor; but when you go inside you will discover it has bedrooms and a bathroom on the second floor level also! It's not a Cape Cod, because there are no windows or dormers that can be seen from the road. You will live in this house just a few years less than you will have lived in your present house.

"You will be continually searching for that ultimate happiness, but you will not really be happy until after your work with your present company is finished.

"I see a rainbow above your head and I can see a word written on the rainbow, but I can only make out the first two letters, a 'C' and an 'A'—It could spell California—or it could be the name of a town in the southern part of the state where you now live. Do you live in Ohio?" "Yes, yes I do." *Big deal. My car out front has license plates on it*, I thought.

"Well," she went on, "if it is California, it appears it will be in the San Diego area, on the road that leads to Mexico.

"Wherever it is, I see a machine shop, and you will be the owner, and I see something about 'Gas,' and a lot of, like trailers and cars about. Perhaps like a gas station and trailer lot—or used-car lot, or something of the sort—in conjunction with the machine shop.

"When the time comes for you to make this move, I see you loading up a trailer of some kind, perhaps a 'U-Haul.' You are loading the things most precious to you, that you don't want to part with. I see a vehicle with which you will tow this trailer—it's like a truck and yet it's like a car, sort of a station wagon, but it's a truck. I don't understand that—but it's what I see and I see it as either green or a brownish color.

"In the fifty-eighth or fifty-ninth year, you will bury someone... again the wry smile—and then you will remarry." *Oh, oh! Oh, oh!*

I could think of only one person whose burial would lend itself to remarriage.

Again she interrupted my thought digression. "Remember, I told you these things can be changed with prayer."

You must remember that at the time this was happening I was twenty-nine years of age, and the year was 1956. *What does she mean, I wondered, fifty-eighth or fifty-ninth year...does she mean 1958 or 1959— Good Lord! I hope not. Maybe she means when I am fifty-nine years old and Peg will be fifty-eight years old. Well, that's thirty years away. I'm not going to worry about that now*, I thought. But I didn't like it. I didn't like knowing about it, and having it to worry about.

Now Christina told me that I would one day find myself suddenly possessing a large amount of cash—more cash that I had ever dreamed of owning—and I would be faced with the dilemma of how to invest it.

She just smiled again and said, "Gold. Black gold. Do you know what that is? It's oil—oil and gas. Invest your money in oil and gas wells, and by the time your hair turns to silver, you will be a very wealthy man."

She then paused again, looked seriously concerned, and said, "Arizona. Don't go to Arizona—or you will lose everything!"

That is essentially all I can remember of the reading, all the high points. It took a good two hours of time. When it came time to pay for this, Christina said, "Whatever you wish to give me will be fine but don't give me more than you can afford."

I handed her seven dollars. She counted it, smiled, and said, "I think this is more than you can afford. Don't you want some of it back?" She was right—it was more than I could afford, but I assured her it was all right, and that even that was not enough. I never saw Christina again, but she will always live on in my memories and my life—as you can well imagine, as you read how the prophecy was lived out.

Peg was indeed pregnant, we found out about a month after the reading. Jim was born August 25, 1956. We prayed long hours that he would not be stillborn. When I first saw James Walter Cameron, he was a pathetic seven and a half-pound lump of hamburger. His head was misshaped and badly marked and bruised, apparently from surgical instruments, (forceps or whatever). The doctor assured me that both mother and son were fine. It had been a little difficult, which he attributed to Peg's diminutive stature, but he assured me that everything was "fine."

Upon our first trip to the pediatrician, when Jim was three weeks old, we got the jolt of jolts.

This no-nonsense, no-personality humanoid, masquerading as a doctor, looked at us sternly and queried, "Ever heard of Hydrocephalus?" I had and responded, "You mean, water on the brain?" "Yes, that's exactly what I mean. You're going to have to bring him in here once each week so I can chart his head growth. Can't you see his head's too large?" he asked bluntly. Well, all babies have large heads—how were we to know? This turned out not to be true about the hydrocephalus, but Jim did, indeed, have learning and motor control problems and Jim's life, in and of itself, is yet another book, but through thick and thin, tough love and rocky roads, Jim has made it. And now at age thirty-five, lives alone in a small mobile home six miles from here, where he gets a small social security check and works part time in a supermarket—and the only thing that really upsets Jim is a day off from work.

If everyone in this world could accomplish according to their abilities the way Jim has, it would be a marvelous world indeed.

Scott Andrew Cameron was born June 4, 1965 and he was extremely difficult to raise. We will not invade Scott's personal life anymore than that, as much as I might like to go into that in detail. We will not invade his privacy. He is a joy indeed. He is truly "my beloved son, in whom I am well pleased."

He grew up loving trains, busses and airplanes, took a part time job as driver for campus bus service at Kent State University, and decided after three years that college was not for him, and searched the country for a job as a bus driver. Failing that he entered the airline industry, and is now very happy, doing rather well, considering everything, working for one of the major airlines, and is about to make his first significant move, up the corporate ladder.

So once again Christina was right on target. All the job predictions and transfers proved to be exactly as she had foretold in my case.

My brother, who had been in Africa during the War, was now head of the Agricultural Department of the State University of New York Campus, at Alfred, New York. He had recently earned his doctorate in the Animal Sciences from Cornell University.

While we were visiting his family in Alfred, where he now had a large farm as well, he informed us that he was soon to be leaving Alfred, as he had obtained a position with the A.I.D. Program, and would be moving to Ghana, Africa for "a few years."

Well Christina did it again. That stretched into ten years and a move to Ethiopia, where revolution raged, and as he was living just across the street from Emperor Haili Salassi's royal palace, actually witnessed the Emperor's kidnapping.

Charles was faced with the dilemma of signing on for another two years when I entered into a pact with his eldest daughter, Marianne, to pray this situation to a satisfactory conclusion—and we did.

On New Year's night, while we watched our beloved Penn State Nittany Lions win the Orange Bowl game, Charles informed me thusly, "Walt," he said, "do you know that you and Marianne were responsible for my decision to come back home, and to S.U.N.Y. (State University of New York)?" Well, enough said. That fulfilled that one.

One evening in June, at a gab fest following a Ham Radio Club meeting, I was chatting with one of the ham's, Doc Willoughby, a medical doctor in Warren. Doc was talking about having met the daughter of one of my best friends, at an art museum in Germany, and what a coincidence it was to meet someone he knew in Europe. I lamented, "I'd like to go to Europe sometime, but it doesn't look like I ever will now." At which he said, "Don't say that. You never know—something could come up tomorrow morning that would cause that to change." I thought that was a strange comment but I took it philosophically.

Next morning I was called into the general superintendent's office at 8:00 A.M., and advised to get my passport immediately. "We are sending you to Luxembourg on the blast furnace rebuild job." I went, stayed a week and came back,. Three weeks later I went again, this time with my wife along, and with the general superintendent himself. Peg and I stayed in Europe another ten days after the business was ended and had a lovely experience—seeing Paris, Zurich, Luzerne, and London before returning home.

I had indeed been "sent across the water twice," by my employer, on company business. *Wow!*

Strange as it seems, I had a sort of loss of memory of these things until they came about. Then I would remember vividly the prophesy of each event. I presume this to be a mechanism built in to prevent my forcing things to happen.

I now have to go back to 1972, when we were getting frustrated with the school system in Warren. Our Jim needed to be in "special education" or EMR classes, as they were then known, "educatable mentally retarded" classes.

Warren, although a small town with about sixty-five thousand people, was racially divided. The civil rights movement was in full swing, so there were some very understandable frustrations, and problems for the community and the schools. All too often when a minority child became a discipline problem, or had a "social" learning problem, rather than deal with them properly, in an understanding and caring way, the school officials simply sent all discipline and learning problem children to Special Education—as one would do with anything deemed to be unusable—just put it aside.

So Jim was in the special education program and a whole building. The old Market Street High School was devoted to junior high and high school-age "EMR's." Everyday Jim's lunch money was taken from him, and he had to wear his boots and overcoat all day long— the only way to avoid having them stolen. It was a real tragedy, but Warren's problems were social and Jim's problems were different than that, so we sought to find a rural place to live where Jim could find education, rather than frustration.

One day a real estate broker telephoned and asked if we wanted to sell our house. This fit right in, and before we could turn around twice and catch our breath, our house was sold.

We now had a few months for the buyers' loan to go through, plus thirty days from closing to find a house and move out.

Time was passing rapidly and we were getting nowhere in finding a suitable house in our price range. Only then did I discover that we had moved too quickly—and sold our house at much too low a price—no wonder it went on the first showing.

One night, when I was particularly troubled, I could not sleep. I tossed and turned, and worried. I had put thousands of dollars and many, many hours of labor into this house, making it just right and now—stupid jerk that I am—I had sold it. It wasn't mine any longer. I had to move out and I had no place to go. Cold sweat, fear, trepidation. *What to do? Pray! Yes, Dear Lord, help me. What am I going to do? I've sold my house and have no place to go. Help me Lord.*—I stopped my mental prayer and almost "heard" a still, small voice ask me, "Where is your faith?" *I'm sorry Lord, forgive me for worrying. I know you are in control.* My peace passed all understanding and I fell asleep.

A day or so later, a phone call came for me at the office. It was Peg. "Sorry to bother you at work, Dear," she said, "but I saw a pretty nice house today with Gerry Challenger (our sales representative, who was trying to locate a house for us), and if you'd like, we can make an appointment to go through it tonight." "Okay," I said, "let's do it. Seven o'clock. Fine. We'll go look at it."

We didn't know that the lady who lived in the house was a little eccentric, and even though she and her husband were building a new home, which was about ready for occupancy, she would not allow any agents to bring potential buyers into the house. So several brokers had already "dropped" her as an unwilling seller; but that night she happened to be out of the house and her husband politely showed the house. Just as we were finishing up in the kitchen about to enter the attached garage, the lady arrived; she pulled into the garage in her Volkswagen Beetle, bounced into the kitchen, and immediately upon seeing Gerry and Peg and me, began to rave and physically beat on poor Gerry, for having brought us into her house.

It was too late. We had already seen it and made an offer. Our first offer rejected, we made a second, and with it bought ourselves a house.

It was a brick house, exactly 300 feet outside the city limits, in Howland Township. From the street, the house looked like a ranch house, but a full-length "dutch dormer" on the rear made for two huge bedrooms and a half bath on the second floor—to go along with the two bedrooms and bath on the first floor. Honestly, it did not occur to me until months after we moved in that this was precisely the house Christina had described.

We had lived in our first house nearly nineteen years, we would live in this house just short of sixteen years. And even the terms of the ultimate sale had been foretold by Christina accurately, although I haven't detailed that here.

What about the rainbow—the letter "C" and "A"—the California bit? Or was it Southern Ohio—a city beginning with the letters CA? Well, you decide.

Don Anderson was a high school guidance counselor, and married to Peg's sister, May; so Don and I often had discussions about both Jim and Scott, he very generously offering the benefit of his expertise in guiding teenagers.

I had once said to Don that I felt the ideal solution for our situation was for me to find a place in the country, where I could have a shop, possibly a small machine shop, and raise food on the land. Possibly Jim could help raise the crops, sell some at the roadside, and help me in the shops. Thus we solved the problem of Jim's future. It sounded good and one day Don gave me a clipping of a classified ad he had cut from the *Akron Beacon Journal* which read:

> For Sale, country estate farm, with complete operating machine shop, living quarters, barn, pond, sixty-three acres, three mobile home pads, hookups for travel trailers, and leased out for drilling gas or oil wells. All mineral rights included.

I got so excited I could hardly contain myself. I called the realtor, who informed me the property was in southern Ohio, just outside Cambridge, Ohio. Further research revealed the asking price to be just a little less than the amount of my lump sum pension benefit, plus my invested savings program money.

We made numerous trips to the place, became rather friendly with the owners, and even took our camping trailer down several times and stayed overnight on the place.

The owner had a nice little business going—just exactly the kind of business I was best at. And he had one full-time machinist working in the shop. This was it—the "CA," the southern Ohio, the machine shop, the trailers. The gas, I figured, was the yet-to-be-drilled gas wells. I was excited. We made an offer, deliberately contingent on the sale of our home, to allow thinking time and family discussion time and also to allow the "forces to work." If it was meant to be, our house would be sold and Christina would be right on target again. But, there was only one member of the family really enthusiastic about the move and as time passed I realized that Peg and the boys really did not like it and our house didn't sell, and so it passed.

But to me, that was the place described by Christina. She didn't say it was definite anyway.

By the way, we now owned a travel trailer and had purchased a Chevy Suburban for towing the trailer. The suburban was green.

Suburbans were not yet in existence when Christina described the car that was a truck that looked like a station wagon. But I now owned one and no description ever offered can better describe a Suburban.

Soon after, we ended up owning several more Suburbans—brown ones, metallic brown, with cream-colored side panels.

However, when we finally packed up to move out of that house, we owned, and still do own, a blue Suburban, which Christina had not mentioned.

And now, for the biggie—one day, after having visited our family doctor, Peg came home (she was fifty-eight years old at the time) and said our doctor wanted her to see a cardiovascular specialist. While examining her, our family doctor put the stethoscope to Peg's neck, and didn't get the sound he should have. There was something wrong in the carotid arteries.

This fifty-eighth or fifty-ninth year prophecy was one that had bothered me a lot through the years and now it was here. Peg was fifty-eight. I was fifty-nine and we had a problem.

The specialist did an angiogram, and determined surgery was needed immediately on Peg's right Carotid Artery. The blockage was so severe she was in imminent danger of a stroke.

He explained the risks. The success rate was about ninety-five percent for the surgery. Three were "some risks," among which was that of having a stroke during surgery.

He was a very thorough, and again, in a reassuring way, stressed the ninety-five percent success rate. In his opinion, Peg's risk of a stroke without the surgery was almost a certainty—about ninety-five percent.

The decision was that we had no choice. All the numbers pointed to surgery being a must.

This part of Christina's prophecy I had never uttered to anyone that I can recall, especially Peg, so I worried alone—and prayed and prayed—and called my daughter, who lived sixty-five miles away, near Cleveland. I insisted she come to see her mother, even though she was taking the procedure very lightly, as young people are prone to do. Her many duties as a young mother were finally put aside in favor of a visit to her own mother, and of course, being a devout, born-again Charismatic Christian, she would pray for her mother.

Our family doctor, a man about my age who had emigrated from Germany, is a very personable, friendly man, with a very matter-of-fact philosophy on life, and he didn't make me feel a lot better when I was explaining to him that I felt the ninety-five percent success rate was pretty good odds. He said, "Yah, dat's goot, but if you are one of da five percent, den it's one hundred percent for you." (Thanks a lot, doc.) But I knew what he meant.

Peg came through one hundred percent fine, has been better than ever, ever since, and again, I believe, without prayer changing things—it could well have turned out the other way. But it didn't, and believe me, both Peg and I have had the best years of our lives since that operation. I am so very glad to have that one behind me, and thankfully, prayfully corrected.

The next item of the reading, I'm sure, has you wondering by now, for you already know I am living in Arizona as I write this and Christina said,"Whatever you do, don't go to Arizona." Well, I've solved that one.

In 1981 on a vacation trip west, we stopped to visit my sister and her second husband, who were now living in the copper mining town of Bagdad, Arizona.

My brother-in-law needed to go to the company offices for some personal affairs, and invited me to go along.

As a joke I said, "Sure, I'll go along, maybe I'll get a job while we're at the employment office and I'll move to Bagdad too."

He said, "You can try, but they are not hiring now." I said, rather cockily, "They'll hire me."

So while there, I stepped up to the window labelled "Employment" and addressed a young lady seated behind the counter.

"I'd like to fill out an employment application," I said to her.

She replied, "We aren't hiring." I shot back, "Oh, you'll hire me all right."

"Oh, yes?" she responded, "And why is it you are so sure of that?"

"Well, young lady, when yo hear my credentials and my work record, you will not be able to turn me away."

At that moment a head popped through the door to the adjacent office, and a woman a little older, and obviously with some authority was speaking to me. "Would you come in here please," she asked. "I'd like to ask you some questions."

After having talked for a while, she sent me out into the mill and the mine area to be interviewed by the respective managers. They told me they had no immediate need for any one with my qualifications, but that they would have in approximately one year and they did not want me to get away. If I was willing to hire on as a mechanic or millwright, they would start me at $11.00 per hour and I could have the job. They wondered about the great drop in wages from what my present position was paying.

I explained that my lump sum pension benefits and the earnings from my invested pension, plus my wages, would probably be more money than I was presently being paid.

Satisfied, they advised me to report to the company hospital at 8:00 A.M. the next morning for a physical examination. If I passed that, they would allow me six weeks to get my affairs in order and report for work.

I had a hernia which I had not known about. The doctor told me I must have it repaired before going to work. So home we went, and the first day back to work I had a new problem. I was being offered a new position in Youngstown, Ohio, at the pipe mill. I dutifully responded to my boss. If this was a genuine opportunity for me and if the company really needed me for this job, then I would accept it. I informed him of the Arizona situation—and the hernia.

He said, "Go get your hernia fixed and come back to work. We really do need you for this position."

One year later the job for which I was transferred was canceled as a result of rising oil prices, and the most serious business recession, in the steel industry history. I, along with hundreds of others, having over the necessary thirty years toward retirement, was let go—at age fifty-five. What a traumatic blow it was, but we survived it.

Meanwhile in Arizona, copper prices had crashed, the mine had been closed down, and the new project they proposed had been canceled. I would have left jobless, if I had taken that job. (And, as it turned out, that one year that had elapsed allowed my pension to increase about fifty percent.) So I'm very satisfied that that was the Arizona move I was not to make—and I did not.

The only thing left was Christina's advice to invest in "black gold," so, for the first time since the reading, I allowed myself to be governed by the reading. I went to Paine-Webber and put most of my pension money in oil and gas—and lost a bundle.

But I have lived as well as ever since retirement. Oil and gas, along with Social Security, has sustained me. And in true family tradition, my hair is still dark, just now showing signs of some silver. So maybe the oil and gas will pay off yet one day.

Christina said it would.

CHAPTER XVII
THERE'S YOUR KITCHEN

I don't quite know how to set up the remaining episodes, though it really doesn't matter, since they are isolated, individual events and the chronology is not all that important. So I'll begin with what I deem to be the most difficult to tell, and that is what I call the "kitchen episode."

Most of the remaining events occurred during the time we lived in the first house. That would be from 1953 until May of 1972.

After having lived in the Forest Street house for several years, we became enamored with the idea of remodeling the kitchen; so we went to look at kitchens at a fine quality "House of Kitchens." We really like the style of the new cabinets they had just placed on display in the front window of the store. They were the famous "Quaker Maid" cabinets, and set on display in the form of a complete kitchen, complete with a peninsula counter and look-through cabinets about the peninsula. We love it, although the layout was in no way similar to our own kitchen. So the salesman measured our kitchen and made a proposed layout to suit our measurements, using the same cabinet design that we had selected, the one on display in the window.

When the proposal was ready, the salesman called us; we made an appointment and went in to confer with him.

Well not much of a conference was needed. The price was nearly half what we had paid for the entire house and we could not presume to afford this, so we put it on the back burner for a few years.

Eventually I suggested to Peg that we could buy a six or eight-foot wide cabinet—a sink unit and put a few wall cabinets above. This we could do for three or four hundred dollars (I thought) and it would be an improvement and might help make the house more salable, should we decide to sell. It sounded good to Peg, so I set out looking. I will not go into detail as to some of the strange things that I encountered—such as crabby sales people, short inventories, all kinds of things that interfered with my ability to close a deal and buy the cabinets. Finally after three or four months of trying to buy cabinets with no success, I told Peg I was giving it up. "It seems something is trying to prevent me from buying these cabinets," I said to Peg. "I'm not going to fight it any longer. I give up. We'll forget about the kitchen." (Peg never disagrees.)

Sometime soon after we had given up, an ad appeared in the newspaper, placed by the company that had made the first proposal-fifty to seventy-five percent off on display kitchens, even more on some. In the ad was a photograph of the storefront window, showing the kitchen we had liked so much some years before.

The same cabinets were still in that window. So I said to Peg, "Let's go have a look."

On our arrival at the store, all the sales people were already busy with other bargain hunters. We were told someone would be with us as soon as possible. I said, "Okay, I'll just go ahead and do some measuring. I now had every dimension of my kitchen committed to memory.

The more I measured, the better it got. If I would turn the kitchen ninety degrees to the right and cut off the peninsula area, it would fit our window wall, and with some other juggling around...most of what we needed was right there and would fit perfectly with only one small vacant space.

By now the salesman had arrived, I pointed out the units I needed, with the sink and counter tops and the gas range included.

I explained the one vacancy. He said, "No problem. They are still building this cabinet design and I can order a new one for that spot." Well it seemed perfect. Now, for the ringer. How much was this going to cost. "Well, everything complete, including gas range and installation...will be $950.00, tax included."

This we could not pass up. The order was placed and a week or so later the kitchen installed, save for plumbing, which I had agreed to do.

On the day of installation, I could hardly wait to get home from work and as I entered the house, Peg said, "The kitchen man was here and he said that he had installed hundreds, maybe thousands, of kitchens in his lifetime, but never had he ever installed any that fit as perfectly as this one does."

As I grasped Peg around the waist, and walked her toward the kitchen, to get my first glimpse of the new cabinets, I took her through the dining room. And at the very moment my eyes beheld the beautiful cabinets, I gasped—a gasp of a mixture between horror and utter disbelief. Peg looked up at me. "What's wrong? Are you all right?" she asked. "I'm not sure," I answered. "You had better sit down while I tell you this, because you are not going to believe it." I knew she *would* believe it because she would know I was telling the truth, but nevertheless I was shell shocked: I now remembered an experience I had several years ago—and had forgotten.

It happened as I was on the way home from attending a retirement banquet, held for one or two fellow employees, now retired. As was our usual custom, we held these at the "Cafe 422," a fine place a half mile or so down the road from the kitchen center.

At the party we had pre-dinner cocktails, then dinner, then a little ceremony honoring the retirees. Then those who wished could remain, play cards, socialize and have a few drinks.

It is important to the story to advise you that I had as many as possibly three beers during the entire affair. Now three beers usually have no more effect on me than a nice tranquilizer would have but, in any case, three beers, two of which would have been before dinner.

At about 9:00 P.M. or thereabouts I got into my car to drive home, and soon after leaving the restaurant parking lot, my lights caught the kitchen in the window and a silent voice spoke to me and said, "There is your kitchen." I silently spoke back and said, "Not my kitchen." The silent voice again spoke, "Oh, yes. That will be your kitchen—not one like it, but that one—the one in the window."

Well this was too much and I said "That's silly, that kitchen will never fit in my house." The voiceless voice shot back, "Oh, we'll make it fit perfectly." With that, I silently answered, "Yeah. Well how about the price? I'll never be able to afford it." And the voice again said, "We will get it for you for less than one thousand dollars." With that I shouted very loudly, "Well then, more power to you. Go ahead and get it." I went on home, went to sleep, and never remembered this incident again—until the exact moment I laid eyes on that kitchen, which had fit so perfectly in our house, which was the exact same one that was in the window, and which cost me $950.00—under one thousand dollars. At the risk of whatever consequences telling a story like this might bring, I tell it, with full knowledge that there are no witnesses, but with my assurance to you that this is as true as any gospel truth can be. It happened—just like that—and no one can ever take that away from me. I know there is someone out there somewhere, that there is another dimension to this life—and I have experienced it.

And my trusting, ever-loving wife Peg knows it is the truth because she has the most astounding ability to read my every thought and when I ever attempt to sway away from the truth, she knows it.

CHAPTER XVIII
SIX MONTHS TO LIVE

During our early married years we became acquainted with several young couples, who all became fast friends for life. Among them were Bob and Ireta. We met this couple when our respective daughters were playing together at a Sunday school picnic and decided that it would be nice if their parents could meet each other as well. So along came these four and five-year-old children to make introductions all the way around. And the tots were right. I guess Peg's best friend in the whole world today is still Ireta.

There are many more, who are nearly as close, but Ireta has the edge on any of the rest by a nose.

Along about July 4, 1968 or 1969 (I'm not sure which), Bob and Ireta had invited us to their country place for a July 4th picnic.

Bob was a very accomplished electrical engineer, who had been on lengthy assignments all over the world, overseeing the installation of steel mill equipment built by his company, Wean Engineering Company.

Bob was three or four years older than I, Ireta the same age as I. Peg and I were the youngest of the couples in the circle of friends.

Bob and Ireta had happened upon a seventeen-acre wooded ravine, with rippling brook running through, in a beautiful setting in Parkman, Ohio, about twenty miles west of Warren. They planned to one day build their retirement home on this land, but for now it had only a make-shift switchback lane—a road that Bob had carved out of the hillside—and a concrete block barn at the bottom, on the only flat piece of ground on the property.

A tractor and some woodsman tools were housed in the barn. Only the tractor could negotiate the homemade switch back road.

Halfway up the ravine was a nifty little flat, just big enough for a nice campfire and a half dozen or so people to sit around it. On the ledge is where we ate our July 4th hamburger and hot dog picnic, with Coca Cola and toasted marshmallows. The girls had now finished with high school and were dating. One or so of the boy-friends showed up at the picnic. Otherwise it was just the two families.

After eating, Bob invited me to help him dam up the creek. He had selected several places to strategically dam up the creek and reinforce the bank sides, using the abundance of rocks that lay in the stream bed.

"Come on Walt. Let's build a dam," Bob shouted. So, down in the ravine we went and started tossing boulders. Suddenly this non-voice *something* said to me, "He's got only six months to live." I ignored it and passed it off as some crazy thought of my own origin; but soon again it was repeated.

As we worked throughout the afternoon and worked our way downstream, building stone dams along the way, this non-voice repeated at least four or five times, getting more and more insistent, and finally saying, "Listen to me. I'm telling you: he has only got six months to live." I was bothered but still passed it off as part of my own lack of mental stability or something and soon I forgot all about it as, for some strange reason, these things seem always to be forgotten to be recalled at a later date. Ironically this is very similar to some folks' alleged U.F.O. encounters.

The experience was forgotten, and as New Years Eve approached, Peg and I thought it would be nice if three couples of us got together, with our kids, and had a little New Year's Eve party. I phoned the other couple. They agreed to come if we could get Bob and Ireta also. For some reason, we both wanted it to be all three couples.

I called Bob and Ireta's home. No answer. I called the other couple back. They, too, had tried to reach them, but to no avail.

We decided they must have gone to their ravine to go sled riding down the hand-carved road.

This being the case, all bets were off and the deal was scrubbed. No New Year's Eve party.

It was either New Year's Day, or the day following (I can't really remember which) the newspaper arrived, and as my usual custom, I opened to the obituary column first. There was a large photo of

Bob with accompanying headline Robert _____, Engineer dies suddenly.

Bob had been sled riding indeed with his wife and daughters (three now) on that cold, cold night, and at the bottom of one of the rides Bob had some kind of a seizure, which was caused by an aneurism above the right eye, as I recall.

I almost fainted with horror, and hated to show it to Peg, for—other than myself, I guess—Bob was a man of whom she was very fond, as a person, of course, not romantically, but nevertheless it was a very difficult loss to endure.

Ireta went ahead and build that dream retirement home, at the top of the ravine. She lives there today justly proud of her many accomplishments, and still making exciting plans for the future of her very special property.

Whoever-or whatever-that was, that *something* that told me he had six months to live was exactly right. From July 4 to January 2 is pretty darned close to six months.

I have no idea why I should be the recipient of such morbid information, or what useful purpose or benefit it could serve. I certainly wasn't going to tell anyone of my experience—especially Bob or Ireta. But then, after it happened, what of it? It was years before I ever got around to telling Ireta of my experience. And only then for the purpose of assuring her that it didn't really matter that they went sledding on that cold night and that it took hours for the old Amish neighbor to hitch up his team and log sled to go down that ravine and bring Bob out. None of that mattered. Someone, somewhere knew that this was Bob's time, and for some yet un-known and bizarre reason, had chosen to tell me about it six months before it happened.

It was my friend Doc Willoughby who would have the unenviable task of delivering the sad news to Ireta at the hospital that Bob had indeed slipped away. And it happened to have been Bob and Ireta's oldest daughter that Doc Willoughby had bumped into the Art Museum in Germany—small world.

CHAPTER XIX
THE LOST CAR KEYS

In an effort to lighten up just a bit I will interject one of the more recent occasions—that of the lost car keys.

I had purchased a brand-new 1979 Chevrolet Suburban, which was a beauty and a fine Suburban, the only one that Peg ever really liked and enjoyed driving.

When this car was about a year old, and the warranty just about expired, I was still having a fuel problem of some kind, that the dealer could not locate and didn't really believe existed.

Anyway we travelled from Warren, Ohio to Delhi, New York, where Charles was now Dean of the Agriculture Department at the Delhi Campus of S.U.N.Y. On the way, the car gave us some problems, so I took it in to a garage for repairs.

Charles wanted me to go with him to the college farm after lunch on Saturday, so he could plant some garden sweet corn and mow some grass.

We parked near the barn and pulled the barbed wire fence open so we could crawl through, crossed the barnyard to the large garden area, and began dropping corn seed into the holes Charles had previously bored in the ground. We planted all the corn, covered all the seed hills, then mowed the grass around the perimeter of the garden.

At about the time we finished planting, some folks arrived and began chatting with Charles in the center of the garden area. I finished the mowing and waited a while for the chatting to end. While it continued, I noticed a herd of Holstein dairy cows in a field adjacent to where I had been mowing. Being an animal lover, I moved over to the fence and invited the cows over to visit with me. I have always found cows to be sociable creatures, and indeed, these were. They ambled over to the fence and I began to pet one of the larger, more aggressive ones on the face. She seemed to take kindly to this so I slapped her on the flank of the neck, and petted her some more.

The cow and I kept this visit going until I heard Charles call out to me that he was ready to leave.

After dinner we were to deliver my car to the mechanic who would, hopefully, be able to fix the problem. But I could not find my car keys. They were on a key chain with all my keys and were very important to me. I didn't want to lose them. Peg had her spare set, so we took the car to the garage and Charles and I thought that perhaps I had lost the keys while at the farm. So we drove back, covered the entire area as well as possible, with no luck in finding the keys. Wouldn't you know, two more people came along to talk with Charles, almost in the same spot as he had chatted previously.

I continued to look for the keys and finally gave it up as a lost cause. Charles still chatted, so I went back to the fence to visit my cow again. She ambled over to the fence, and as I reached to pet her nose, she stepped back shook her head, and walked about fifteen feet down along the fence. I thought, *All right. I'll play your little game.* I walked over and attempted to pet her again and she repeated the first performance. So did I, again and again, about six times. She kept moving me down that fence, until she finally stopped and seemed content to permit me to pet her. Just about now Charles called to me and asked, "Hey Walt, did you find your keys yet?"

As I started to say, "No, I haven't," my instincts caused me to first look to the ground. There, lying dead center between my feet, were my car keys.

I called out to Charles, and he saw me bend down and pick them up.

I'll never know if that was the exact spot where I had previously petted the cow or not, but no matter. Whether knowingly or unknowingly, that cow had led me to the exact spot where my keys were lying—and I am *not lying*. That's just how it happened.

CHAPTER XX
THE MECHANIC ON THE HILL

The car trouble I was having in the preceding chapter actually began during a small family reunion. It has been a rare thing when all four of us—Bob, Edith, Charles and myself—have been able to be together all at one time.

We were assembled at my home in Ohio, since Edith was visiting from Arizona. Charles had come from New York State, and Bob from North Carolina for the occasion.

Edith always wants to visit the old farm (my birthplace) when she comes East; so we all decided on a picnic at the farm.

It's about a three-hour drive from Warren, Ohio and is not too far out of the way for either Bob or Charles, on their routes homeward, so I agreed to drive over and meet them all at the farm. Edith would then return to Ohio with me, and Bob and Charles would go on their way home.

As I was climbing the last mountain (or hill to some folks) before reaching the old farm road, my car began to buck, then stall, but I was able to "nurse it" up the hill and to the farm.

After the picnic I assured Bob and Charles that I would have the problem taken care of, and that Edith and I would be able to make it back to Warren, Ohio safely.

It had been a lovely time, enjoying the farm. All the buildings had been destroyed by fire years ago; but the land was there, the old lane was there, as were the old spring, the pear and walnut trees and some of the old orchard, so we picnicked and dallied longer than we should have.

It was about 3:00 P.M. on Sunday afternoon when we started home. Edith and I drove into Johnstown, thinking it would provide a better chance to have the car looked at, and Edith also wanted to see some of the old neighborhood, where we had lived.

The vehicle acted all right on the way, since it's all down hill into Johnstown, but once we were there the problems started. I went to Abie Labarko's garage in Oakhurst, since Abie and I had been childhood friends and playmates. Abie could not find anything wrong I felt the problem was the fuel pump (which ultimately it turned out to be) but Abie couldn't accommodate any major repair on a Sunday, so we went on, about three blocks, until the car stalled again. We were near another garage when we stopped, so we tried again. This time the man told us we should go back into Johnstown a few miles to a place he recommended. We did so, but all we succeeded in doing was waste more time, because after the car cooled down a little, it would always start again. I suggested the problem might be a pinched fuel line or poorly operating fuel pump restricting the gasoline flow, and the engine heat then causing a "vapor lock." Well, at the garage, after waiting an hour or so, the car had cooled down and was working fine. The mechanic said if I wanted him to "tear into it," I would have to wait until Monday or Tuesday. I said Edith, "Let's just try to make it. We'll drive till it stops, then let it cool down, and go on. We might not get home until after midnight, but I thought we could get home.

We decided to start home and to ask the Lord to help us—so that we *could* get home. Sis and I never have been failed by the Lord, whenever we have called on him to help us out of a pinch. We went along Highway 56 through the Conemaugh gap and came upon a roadblock. There was some kind of construction, or repair work and the road narrowed to one lane with a flagman directing traffic. This was all we needed—a traffic jam on a hot afternoon. I was afraid to shut off the engine, for fear it wouldn't start again, but I knew the engine heat would shut us down if we had to wait in line too long.

I said to Edith, "We must not have prayed right, or this would not have happened. This is like Murphy's Law."

Edith answered right back, "Just relax. There must be some reason for this delay. Maybe there is someone up ahead who can fix the car, and the Lord wants us to be there at the right time."

I had to accede to this line of thinking, but it wasn't easy. The car didn't stall and we finally got through the construction work and all was well, until we got to a large hill near the township schoolhouse.

The car stalled on the hill and would not start. I let it coast back down the hill where I backed into the school driveway. It would not start so I just waited until it cooled down.

Finally it started again, and we got about half way up the (several-mile-long) grade, when it stopped again. I got it to the side of the road and parked it against the guard rail. We waited for a while for it to cool, but this time it would not start. I had run the battery down and now we were in a real pickle.

Edith began getting concerned, since we were now out in the boondocks, the schoolhouse was closed and nobody was around. We began to walk up the hill, leaving the Suburban sit by the side of the road. We came upon a few houses, but could get no response at any of them. Traffic was whizzing past at a more than moderate rate, and the wind from the passing vehicles could almost have blown us over. People stared from their cars, but nobody offered to stop.

At the very bottom of the hill was a coal mine truck garage and repair shop. But on Sunday nobody would be around there, so I didn't bother thinking about the mile-and-a-half hike back there.

We were now getting discouraged and sunset was upon us. In those Pennsylvania hills that meant almost immediate darkness.

As we continued walking, Edith began to tire out. She has heart problems and has always had bouts of bronchitis and asthma. I was about to get a panic attack, but just then I noticed that a jeep that had just gone up the hill had turned around and was coming back down.

As the driver in the jeep passed, he looked us over very carefully and kept right on going.

I told Edith I had seen him go up the hill, and now he was back. "He's going to stop and help us," I said.

Edith said, "I think you're right!" The jeep just went on past us, but after he passed the stranded Suburban, he turned around and came back up the hill. He stopped and asked, "Is that your vehicle parked down there?"

"Yes, it is," I said.

"Are you having trouble?" he asked.

"Yes we are," I said explaining it to him.

With that he said, "Well, jump in. I'll take you back down there, and I'll have a look at it."

I told him all that had happened, all that I had learned and what I thought was the problem. I further told him it would take a professional to repair it.

With that he responded, "I am a professional." I'm the mechanic at that coal mine garage at the bottom of the hill. Normally I would not be working on a Sunday, nor would I be working this late, but for some strange reason I felt the need to go to the garage a couple hours ago. I was worrying about something, so I came in and checked it out—otherwise I would not have been here.

After looking over the situation he decided there may be a more serious problem, but he thought he could get us home by simply removing the fuel filter from the carburetor. So this he did and the car started. He test drove it up the hill and it was fine.

I tried to pay him but he smiled and said, "No, I'm a Christian and the Lord wants me to help others. That's why I stopped for you. All I ask is that you pass it on and help someone in need when you are in a position to do so."

You will never convince Edith or me that the Lord didn't make that man become concerned so that he would make that unusual trip to the garage on a Sunday—or that the Lord didn't cause all the frustrating delays we encountered, which just *happened* to place us at exactly the right spot at exactly the right time for that "angel of mercy" to come by and help us.

We got home fine with no further problems, and eventually after becoming very insistent, I was able to convince the dealer from whom I had bought that Suburban, to look into it.

He found that the factory had installed a fuel pump with a bent cam lever and it had never been pumping enough gas, so the dirty fuel filter, and the heat of the engine would close off the gas completely—and the problem was finally solved.

CHAPTER XXI
THE GIRL ON THE PORCH SWING

Quite late one balmy summer night, I was sitting on the front porch swing, probably to enjoy a last cigarette before retiring for the night. (I still smoked cigarettes until 1967 but, in deference to Peg's many allergies and chronic bronchitis, I usually went outside to enjoy my bad habit.)

I noticed that in a neighbor's house across the street and about three houses down the street, there seemed to be some kind of excitement in progress. It was like a party or something, as cars were filling the driveway, and several more cars parked on the street in front of the house. Every window in the house had a light coming from it, even the attic and the basement, it seemed. There were shadows of people milling about in the house, and there appeared to be several people gathered in the enclosed front porch, which was now a sort of sitting room.

We didn't know the folks well and had only a neighborly speaking acquaintance. I did know that they were a very sedate couple, who had only one child, a married son whom, I had heard, was living in California.

I also knew that this had to be something really special, for they were not party people.

As I thought about this and watched the house, with its activity, I recalled hearing that the son had been dating a girl whom he had intended to marry, when they learned of the girl's terminal illness. I never heard what the illness was. I never heard whether they decided to go on with the wedding or not. But it had been the subject of some talk in the neighborhood. As I thought about this I became more certain that they indeed had married, in the face of her almost certain death, and were living in California. Could it be that she had indeed passed away in California and they were having the services in Ohio?

At about the time that I resolved to myself that that must be what had happened; I got this strange feeling that someone had lightly and daintily slipped up onto my porch and sat next to me on the swing.

When these things happen I feel strange and wonder to myself, *Am I making this up? Am I letting my imagination run away with me? There I go getting silly again.*

But then this someone beside me spoke in the unspoken language of psychic phenomena. The non voice said, "Sir, can you help me?" And I very obligingly, silently, replied, "I'll try to if I can. What do you need?" Then the answer came back, "Well, I'm really upset with my family. They are all gathered over there, eating, drinking and visiting, but they ignore me. They walk right past me as if they don't even know I'm there and I haven't done anything to make them angry, I hope. Can you help me?"

I now gave serious consideration to the possibility that I was really going crazy. After all, I was dreaming up quite a scenario here— something I would hesitate to discuss with anyone.

Peg's dad had always said the way to deal with a situation like this, is to give a "test"—try to get some kind of information from the entity which might enable one to document the genuineness of the event.

Having considered all this, I responded, "All right. I think I can help you; but first you must tell me your name." I knew this would be a good test because I had never heard, or known, the name of the girl in question.

Immediately the answer shot back: *My name is Janean.* (I don't remember, at this writing, what the name really was. It may have been Janean). Armed with that bit of information, I then went on to explain to her that she had passed on out of this physical life into her spiritual body, and since life continues, some people are not really aware that the transition has occurred.

"Your family loves you dearly, but they do not know that you are here. They can't see you. They think you are dead. So you must go on, and do whatever it is you need to do over there. I'm sure some-one will come to your aid if you understand where you are."

A quiet peace came over me, I almost heard a sigh, and she said, "Thank you. Now I understand," then she was gone.

When the newspaper arrived the next day I looked to the obituary column, and sure enough, the neighbors' daughter-in-law had passed away, and to my great relief her name was that which she had told me. I related the whole incident to Peg, and thanks to the "test" advised repeatedly by Dana M. Bailey Jr., the event was sealed in my mind as authentic—and quite an experience.

CHAPTER XXII
THE SITTINGS

After Dana Bailey retired from his full-time work at the courthouse, he gradually allowed his furniture business to dwindle away as well. He and Grace sold the big old house in Newton Falls and moved to a house just a few blocks away from where Peg and I lived. They wanted to be near the grandchildren—Grace's "little darlings." She especially loved Jim, probably because she knew Jim need the extra love and attention that only a grandmother could give.

Dana assembled a group of his friends who had expressed an interest in "sitting." They would assemble in Dana's living room, just talk for a while, then have a prayer, sing a hymn or two, almost always including "In the Garden"; then, they would dim the lights and sit quietly, waiting for something to happen. Quite often, nothing happened, but other times things seemed to happen.

The rule was that when anything at all came into your mind, you would talk about it and perhaps determine it to be psychically inspired or if you saw anything, you would tell the others about what you were seeing.

Usually nothing much happened until one of the brave ones would begin—and then it often started flowing.

I was invited to join in and "sit" with them a few times and I did, rather reluctantly, agree to join in.

Before I tell you of the events of one of these meetings, I think you should know about some of the people who attended. I will not tell names except in the case of one married couple, whom I must identify, simply because of the special identity the husband happened to possess.

He was a man about six feet tall, who must have weighed well over 300, maybe 400 pounds. He was huge. He had mopish, bright red hair and his name was Howard Hector.

He was a personal friend of the cartoonist who wrote "Joe Palooka" in the comic strips—and he was the living, breathing model after whom the comic strip character, "Humphry Hector Pennyworth," was modeled.

In the comic strip, Humphry was the friendly, almost childlike handyman, who pedalled around on his "Humphry Mobile," a tool shed built on the back of a huge bicycle. Humphry used the bike to earn his living, pedalling about looking for knives and scissors to sharpen, or any other little nick-nack repair jobs.

The real life Howard Hector was the spitting image of Humphry of the comic strip—or vice-versa. With the blessing and permission of his friend who wrote the comic strip, he also had a Humphry Mobile.

He had constructed a look-alike toolshed mounted over the two rear wheels of a tri-wheel motorcycle. He acquired a wardrobe of clothing the exact duplicate of the comic strip characters and would "hire out" for special appearances at public events.

Parades, street fairs, carnivals, circuses, grand openings, special sales promotions—you name it—Howard was there on his "Humphry Mobile" dressed as Humphry Pennyworth, and everybody loved him. I believe his real job was that of insurance sales, or maybe real estate, something like that. I don't remember exactly. Howard and his lovely, vivacious wife Jan were, in the personality sense, a perfect match, but were physically as opposite as you could get. Jan was a very attractive, shapely, diminutive lady with a bubbling personality, and as I recall—but not with certainty—she had reddish or maybe auburn colored hair.

Another couple, as a sideline, were the owners of a retreat in the mountainous forests of Pennsylvania, where they had prepared landing sites for U.F.O.s or "flying saucers."

There was an authentic Indian chief, who was a show business performer. He displayed his prowess with the pistol and various other skills. He always came dressed in his full "council dress"— and he was beautiful.

There were a few others, who came intermittently, individually or in couples—it didn't matter.

Dana was always there. Sometimes Grace would "sit in," as a spectator I guess, as she never really participated.

I think I attended twice. The first time was pretty much a dud as far as any results were concerned. However the second was different and was enough to cause it to be my last time.

This evening Grace was sitting in. Also there were the Indian chief, Howard and Jan Hector, the friends who owned the retreat in Pennsylvania, another lady who came alone from a nearby town in Western Pennsylvania, and of course, Dana ("Dad") and I as well.

We did the usual Lord's Prayer and sang a few verses of "In the Garden." The Chief played his tom-toms and chanted some songs addressed to the "Great Spirit." Then we sat quietly. After a little quiet meditation, then some brief conversation about ground rules and what might be expected to happen, the room was darkened.

The shades were drawn and only a little light from the street light, out in front of the house, shone through the cracks where the blinds didn't completely close out all the light. It was just enough that you could "almost" make out the forms of the people seated around, but not quite.

We sat and sat. Soon Dana spoke out, "Please folks, if you get anything, don't be bashful. If you see, hear, or think anything, tell us about it. That's the only way we can get any results."

A few people mentioned some of their thoughts. Then it got quiet again, so Dana did a little oratory. (He was very good at story telling.) Then it became quiet again.

I imagined that I saw something, but was reluctant to speak; but then I saw it more vividly and decided to speak up.

"I just saw what appeared to be a black leopard slink across the room and sit on the floor in front of Jan and Howard, then it put one paw on Jan's lap, and laid its head down on her lap as well."

Immediately Dana spoke out, "I saw that too, Walter, but I wasn't sure I was seeing it so I didn't say anything. But what you describe is exactly what I saw." Now I became a little braver and I said, addressing the lady named Jean, "Would you know anything about a brain tumor? Would you know anyone who is suffering with a brain tumor?" She said, "No, I don't know anyone with a brain tumor now, but my father died of cancer of the brain."

I said, "Well, that must be it then. But I still see something about you, something in your neck. Would you mind standing in the middle of the floor and I'll lay my hands on your neck and head?"

Those were the only events that stirred my memory enough from that night to write about. I'm sure there were other subjects, and other things voiced.

After we closed and the lights came on, people began leaving. The couple who owned the retreat hung around until after everybody else had left—except of course Dana, Grace and myself.

"The reason I stayed around" said Ina, (the lady's name is Ina) "is that I want to tell Walter something about what he saw."

"Walter, you probably don't know this, but the black leopard is a very bad omen, and is most often associated with impending doom, so we don't usually say anything when we see that."

Of course I was chagrinned and embarrassed. How could I have known? I only told what I saw.

Ina tried to reassure me and soften my embarrassment, and I pretended to feel better, but I didn't, and no matter what happened, I was never going to do this again. I didn't like the sound of that at all. And besides that, it felt too much like some kind of voodoo or something.

No more of this for me, I thought and I didn't go back again; but the rest of them kept right on going.

In a few months, I was informed that Jan had been diagnosed with "cancer in the abdominal" area and the doctors didn't give her much chance. And so it was that in a year or so Jan died of the Cancer.

Howard still continued to sit and on one evening, when they had all been sitting at a friend's home near Sharon, Pennsylvania, they all agreed to meet afterwards at the El Rio Cafe on the "strip" in Warren, Ohio, for some coffee and dessert.

Dana and most of the group had already arrived, and were assembled around a table with their coffee, waiting for Howard, who was the last to arrive.

Before Howard arrived, the group heard a loud bang-bang near the entrance to the cafe. Someone shouted, "He's been shot. He's been shot."

Dana and some others rushed to the entrance, where, just outside they saw Howard, lying dead on the steps to the entrance way.

Someone had shot him and then disappeared. The murder has never been solved as far as I know, but word is around, that it was a professional mob hit intended for someone else, but imposed upon poor innocent Howard, by mistake.

Jean died of a brain tumor at about the same time that Jan Hector died.

I make no claims. I feel no blame. Certainly I feel terrible to lose such nice people to such horrible deaths; but I also wonder, *What's the sense of it all? What useful purpose can such information have?*— None that I can think of, so why mess with it?

CHAPTER XXIII
VISUALS

For those who are interested in the pursuit of parapsychology or in Spiritualism, the visual or material manifestation is the apex of excitement.

It is for this reason that so many fraudulent mediums provide materialization seances.

I cannot say much on this subject, since I have attended such seances only three or four times, and to my honest interpretation, the results were rather questionable. It is true that some convincing information is transmitted by the visiting "spirits," and also true that something or things, alleged to be spirits, do appear. I was not able to see clearly enough to make any positive identifications in the darkened seance rooms, nor was I comfortable about being there at all when several of my long-deceased relatives stood face-to-face with me and made vague, light-hearted comments, in very general terms.

What bothers me most is that the mediums oblige themselves to provide at least one, and usually two or three, visiting spirits for each paying guest. Usually about thirty people comprise a nice materialization seance group—at anywhere from twenty to one hundred dollars each; at those prices the mediums dare not disappoint anyone.

My wife and other members of her family will solemnly attest that they have seen, with absolute certainty, very identifiable relatives and friends, and even strangers who come as guides, such as Native Americans in full tribal costume or in loincloths, stealthily creeping about the seance room. I will not belittle what I have not seen; but what I have seen has not overwhelmingly convinced me.

The idea that twenty or thirty people can sit in a group, and each one have numerous spirit visitors is just too unbelievable for me. If just one good, solid, verifiable, spirit would appear during the entire seance, I would be more convinced than by the mass production system that guarantees satisfaction to curious, paying guests.

I must admit, though, that it is not all that different from a mass healing service at Charismatic assembly, where hundreds of people ante up thousands of dollars for the "healing touch" of the evangelist and where, also, I have never seen a real bona fide authentic, verifiable example of healing take place (although I'm sure that some have).

I'm not saying to you that I do not believe in the existence of the manifestation of materialization; I not only believe it, I have seen it. What I am saying is that I have seen more in the privacy of my own bedroom, spontaneously, than I have ever witnessed at a seance. My faith is a personal faith and not a public exhibition, and therefore, it is much more profound than the commercial variety, in much the same way, I would imagine, as intimate amorous interludes with one you love, in the privacy of your own room would be much more satisfying than would be the paid services of a prostitute who, in a manner of speaking, "provides the real thing."

It is my firm belief that we all have a sensitivity to the supernatural or, in other words "psychic power," in varying degrees We are just like radios, some of which are not turned on, others which are turned on, but not tuned in. The best way I know to turn on and tune in is by remembering that your psychic radio is not only a receiver, but also a transmitter. The only channel on my radio transmitter is tuned to God, tuned in on the Jesus Christ frequency, for I believe that God the Father Almighty through his son, Jesus, and the Holy Spirit, is the true and only source of life and life eternal.

Prayer is the instrument of contact, in both directions—not only from you to God but also from God to you. If God chooses to send an angel, or ten thousand angels, he will do so. If he chooses merely to whisper a response in your ear, he will do so. If he chooses to use some other symbolic type of message he will do so. It must be our responsibility to recognize that answer and act upon it when it is received.

When you pray, you must always allow some "listening time" after you have finished uttering your end of the prayer, keep on listening and waiting every moment of your life and keep on praying at least once a day, preferably more often.

When you have established a true and sincere faith and a working "radio frequency" to God your answers will come and you will not need to go to the prostitutes of the faith to get your answers.

The several visual experiences that have come to me were so vivid and profoundly clear as to be astonishing, wonderful, and unmistakable.

Among them have been fleeting glimpses of a quickly vanishing apparition, such as one I presume to be of Peg's sister Lily Alice, who would frequently appear at the banister, half way up the semi-open staircase in our Forest Street home.

The most moving, and convincing of all was the unexpected visitation that occurred one night in our bedroom.

During the wee hours of the morning, something awakened me. Peg was sound asleep, beside me in our double bed. Standing beside the bed, on Peg's side of the bed, were the figures of two women. When I first saw this I assumed myself to be still asleep and dreaming it. I undertook to assure myself that I was indeed awake. Next I thought that Peg must have hung a gown over a lamp or something over there which looked like someone standing there. I raised my head just a teeny bit, squinted, and stared and stared—and peered into the two faces.

Yes, they really were there. They had sort of a misty, bluish-white foggy kind of appearance to them and were almost transparent. The one I immediately recognized as Peg's now departed mother, the other looked very much like Peg but had long, flowing hair down her back. They were smiling pleasantly and looking down at Peg, who was still sound asleep on her stomach. I assumed the younger one to be "Lily Alice," a sister of Peg's, who would have been a little older than Peg had she not died soon after birth. Previous encounters by other family members, had indicated that Lily Alice had grown up on the other side, and looked very much like her two still-living sisters, May and Peg.

I now decided that Peg had better see this too, so I very gently, quietly slipped my right hand over and began tapping Peg on the shoulder. She soon stirred and as usual, seemed annoyed at having been awakened, and asked, "What is wrong?"

I whispered, "Shhh! Don't say anything. Just try to look up over you left shoulder."

She caught on immediately and tried to turn her head toward the two apparitions, but the moment she moved her head they vanished. They were gone—just like a cloud that vaporizes before your eyes in a summer sky.

Had I been seeing some object that was standing there, it would not have disappeared. It would still be there to later reveal itself as a lamp or whatever.

This was not the case. What had been there was now gone. I knew who had been there this time—Grace and Lily Alice Bailey. They spoke not a word, sent not a thought. They just stood there, smiling over Peg. Maybe there was some reason for this appearance, but, to my knowledge, it never has been revealed.

On one other occasion, Peg had already gone upstairs to get ready for bed, when I decided to do the same thing. Our stairway was semi-open and climbed the west wall of the living room to a hallway running at right angles to the stairway on the second floor.

The first door on the right was the bathroom. At the end of the hallway on the right was our bedroom. The children occupied the two rooms on the left and they had already been asleep for hours.

As I reached the top of the stairs and turned left to go down the hallway, I noticed the bathroom door was open and the light was on. So, as I passed by, I glanced in hurriedly and saw Peg (I thought it was Peg) standing in front of the mirror—brushing her beautiful, long blonde hair.

I said, "Hi," as I passed the door, and hurried on down the hall to the bedroom. The door to the bedroom was closed and I could see light coming from the crack under the door.

This did not strike me as unusual, as Peg would often leave the bedroom light on and the door closed while she would do whatever it is women do in the bathroom at bedtime.

I opened the door, expecting to see an empty bed, but there was Peg—sitting up in bed reading. I reeled back, shocked, and said, "No. No, you can't be here. You are in the bathroom."

"What in the world are you talking about?" asked Peg.

I raced back down the hallway, there was no light on in the bathroom—and there was no blonde brushing her hair.

I gulped, returned to the bedroom, looked at Peg, and only now realized that Peg had recently had her hair cut short. The hair I saw in the bathroom was long.

Could it have been our daughter Diane? Hardly. Her hair was fire red, only neck length, and she was just a child. Nobody came out of that bathroom and no light switch was heard to click off.

We are quite certain it was Lily Alice again. Why? Who knows, I only know what I experienced. But this time it was not a misty, foggy, transparent thing. It was a person, in living color.

CHAPTER XXIV
DANA'S AND GRACE'S HEART ATTACKS

At about the time Peg's Dad retired from his political position at the courthouse, he became ill, with what was apparently a mild heart attack, which Dana referred to ever after as angina pectoris and for which he would take nitro glycerine tablets and possibly some other medications. He was not hospitalized, but remained in bed at home.

In those days a few doctors still made house calls, so Dana stayed at home. He apparently had the idea that he was going to die at this time, because he was very upset.

On one occasion, when I was visiting alone with him at his bedside he began to cry and he said to me tearfully, "Walter, I'm afraid I'm not going to make it. What do you think?"

At that moment I got another psychic message that said to me "Tell him he'll live to be eighty-seven years of age." At that I smiled and said light heartedly to him, "Nonsense, Dad. They tell me you're going to live to be eighty-seven, perhaps more. (I added the "perhaps more" since I had enough foresight to imagine him reaching age eighty-seven and waiting to die.)

He seemed genuinely relieved, smiled, let out a big sigh, and said, "Thank you Walter. I hope you are correct."

Dana had always believed he was born in the year 1896, and he lived and worked accordingly. But when he was about to retire, there was no birth certificate, so he had to resort to a baptismal certificate, which was made out in 1896. As it turned out, after much digging, the baptismal certificate had been make out two years after the fact, or at least two years after his birth. So Dana now learned he was two years older than he thought. It really didn't matter a whole lot since age sixty-five was retirement age, and in either case, he was past that.

What is interesting is that Dana passed away in September of 1981, at the age of eighty-five—unless the two-year error was correct—in which case he died at age eighty-seven—exactly as I had been told to tell him.

As for Grace Bailey, Dana's marvelous and saint-like wife, we also had a foretelling of her passing. It was Madam Christina who had told Peg, more than ten years prior to Grace's passing. What Christina told Peg was that "when you visit your mother in the hospital and you see that they have her on oxygen, you will know the end if very near."

Grace either had polio when she was a young girl, or a birth defect which severely affected one leg. She was able to function almost normally, with the aid of a cane, but she had that dragging of one leg, typical of polio and well known in those days.

One day while Grace was leaving our home, after visiting her "darlings," she tripped on the stairs leading outside from the kitchen and fell to the sidewalk, about four steps down.

The only complaint she had was that she had hurt her large toe on her "good leg."

This turned out to be a fracture, which was treated by a podiatrist. He put her leg in a cast up to just beneath the knee and sent her home.

Grace was an iron-willed lady and a game as they come, so she just smiled and said to everybody, "I'm just fine. I'll be all right." She tried to function with one leg that was in a walking cast and one that was afflicted by Polio.

The effort was simply too much on her now aging heart, and she had to be taken to the hospital. None of us really thought it to be very serious, but we were relieved that she was being hospitalized, because it would be much easier on her.

When Peg and I visited her, she had been placed in the cardiac care unit and was feeling bright and cheerful.

There was a little plastic hose that passed over her ears and beneath her nose, with two little hoses, one into each nostril, supplying Grace with much needed oxygen.

The monitors showed a very smooth, strong heartbeat and Grace happily talked of being transferred into a "regular room" the next day, so none of us was alarmed—except Peg, who silently worried to herself—and with good reason as it turned out. At 1:00 A.M. the next morning Grace passed over, just after the night nurse asked her,

"How are you feeling, Mrs. Bailey?" Grace answered, "I'm fine, dear," and closed her eyes forever.

So Christina was on target again. It was 1971, and Dana would live on another ten years before rejoining Grace.

CHAPTER XXV
DANA, THE MAN

It would be inappropriate for me not to devote a chapter to my father-in-law, whom I had grown to love and respect through the years.

It was not exactly a love-hate relationship, but it was always a sort of "handle with kid gloves" deal.

He was such an intense man. His every motion and word was profound. He spoke with a bass, authoritative voice, with an air about him that always projected to anyone present, that he was in control. He always had the last word and whatever he said or did was absolutely right. So you did not counter him with opposing opinions, nor did you express doubt when he spoke. And, by God, everyone listened when he spoke or he would inform them all to pay close attention, as he was about to speak. Despite this demeanor, inside was a meek, mild man, a good man—but a dynamic individual. He was at one time an accomplished cornet player, having attended and taught at Berea College in Kentucky, played with the Chautauqua Symphony Orchestra, travelled with a circus, and toured with a road group of thespians playing all the small towns in the Midwest.

His father had a large furniture store and the town undertaking parlor so Dana also learned the ropes of those businesses. He had many tales to tell of ambulance and hearse calls late at night, in the dead of winter, in a horse-drawn ambulance that served also as a body wagon. In those days, furniture and mortuary businesses were often combined, since caskets were made by furniture makers.

After a falling out with his father, Dana started his own furniture business, selling out of his house, and also became involved in politics—everything he did was done with intensity. He was elected mayor of Newton Falls and served several terms during the big depression. He was always compassionate to the underprivileged, and served as mayor accordingly—as he also priced his furniture accordingly.

When I first came to know him he was the chief deputy clerk of courts of Trumbull County, Ohio. He always managed the election campaign of the "Clerk of Courts" and managed his furniture business as well. And as I said before, he was a voracious reader. Each weekend he would take his little family some place—either to a "spook" camp as he sometimes called it, or to relatives over in Altoona or to Chautauqua or some other cultural event.

Peg was well-rounded, for her dad saw to it that she got to all the good events—the air shows with Roscoe Turner, the Ice Capades, the ballet, the opera—the whole nine yards. Peg never missed a circus, a sportsmen's show, a home show. Whatever Cleveland or the surrounding two hundred miles had to offer, Dana went there with his family. Peg was even to the New York World's Fair in 1939.

Where, incidentally, her Uncle Ed Grimminger (who was in charge of Paint Shops at the world famous Altoona Shops of the Pennsylvania Railroad) was on assignment, babysitting the famous S-1 Locomotive that the PRR had built to exhibit at the World Fair.

So this was a unique man. Small wonder he balked at the thought of a poor country boy from Pennsylvania making off with his Margaret; I never heard him call her anything but "Margaret"—although she would much prefer to be just "Peg."

So this was the man, over six feet tall, and hefting a good two hundred or so pounds. He was impressive and commanding. Everything about him was so. I worked with him in the furniture business to some extent. I did most of the delivery and service work, using only Dana's Pontiac station wagon to haul the furniture.

His business was good. His prices were so low, nobody could compete with him and many competitors were very unhappy with him, but his ideals prevailed. He believed what he believed—and he lived and practiced what he believed.

One thing that always was a sore spot with him was what he call "deathbed salvation." He hated that even more than he hated the Catholic Church's "weekend confessions."

He simply could not buy into the theory that you can live the life of a rat—steal, rob, carouse, cheat or whatever—and then, just when you are ready to "cash in," pray to God and receive salvation for eternity.

"Just doesn't make good sense," he would say.

"If you've been a rat all your life, you are going to die a rat. If you've been forgiven at the confessional on Monday, you are now good for another week of good times." That's how he saw it.

And I never heard anybody disagree with him. Nobody disagreed with him—not if they valued their peace and tranquility.

I'm probably about to get into serious trouble with Peg and May now, but what is, is and I must relate it.

I had always had a premonition or hunch that this man, genuine and sincere as he was, also harbored some doubt. That way, down deep, he really believed, or wanted to believe, "this Jesus thing." But there just were too many silly things connected with it and besides, most of the town's drunks and whore mongers were on the Board of Deacons—even the Pastor himself had questionable morals. This of course was a fact well known to most folks, but it just wouldn't be proper to stir up a fuss over a few hypocrites.

So his facts were in order and his reasons sound, as he saw it; nothing was left open for others to question.

When this one-of-a kind individual finally came face-to-face with his own upcoming demise, he was both brave and scared.

The creeping cancer was eating away at his colon but "by the gods," he would say, "I'll never wear one of those bags. There will be no surgery for me. I'll see this thing through, and live with it, for as long as I can." It finally got so bad that he could no longer function, and had to be hospitalized. When he realized the end was near, he finally consented to the surgery. He made it through the operation, but it was too late—the evil of the "big C" had won its inevitable victory, and Dana lay in his hospital bed, with full knowledge that he was within a day or so of entering that mysterious land he had so long sought to probe.

My last visit with him was a beautiful experience. We were alone, he and I. As I stood by his bedside, I reached over the restraining bed rail and held his hand. He smiled, "Hello Walter, I'm glad you came." I'm sure we both knew this would be our last visit in this life.

As I stood there, now silent, holding his husky hand, he looked up at me and said, "Would you pray for me, Walter?" "Sure Dad," I said and together this giant of a man humbled himself and we prayed together in what is known to Charismatics as the "sinner's prayer." We prayed to Jesus Christ for forgiveness and understanding for this man—who less than twenty-four hours later would cross over that historic bar into his eternal destiny.

The most peaceful smile came onto his face, and he said, "Thank you Walter. I love you."

I said "Good-bye, Dad," and tearfully, yet ever so joyously, walked out of the hospital room.

Dad was either eighty-five or eighty-seven years old when he "died. Yet to this day, I sometimes recall the less pleasant days and think about some of the things about this man that I hated. But this is my sin, my cross to bear and I must learn to forget these things and dwell on the beauty and love of this dear man.

CHAPTER XXVI
HELPFUL HENRY

After we sold our home in the township outside of Warren, we moved into a second-floor apartment in Kent, Ohio.

Each unit of the complex had eight separate apartments, four on each of two levels. Both entrances to each unit were kept locked at all times, so you not only needed your door key to enter your own apartment, but also you needed a key to unlock the outside entrance doors.

There was, living in the first-level apartment adjacent to the front entrance way, an elderly retired couple.

The husband, seemingly for the lack of anything better to do, was always peeking out of his window or apartment door to see what might be going on. If he should see someone coming up the walk-way, he would always dash out of his apartment to open the door for them, or if he heard footsteps in the hallways he would pop out of his door to render any assistance he could, such as opening doors, or just being friendly.

Peg and I, privately and in good humor, referred to him as "Snoopy" or "Helpful Henry." We laughingly enjoyed seeing him pursuing his obvious pleasure. We also wondered if we could ever quietly sneak up on the entrance and thus, undetected, be able to use our own key to open the door, but it never happened, unless he was not at home, which was not often.

Then it began to happen. For a period of about a week I began to catch fleeting glimpses of a peek-a-boo type manifestation inside our apartment on the second floor. After about a week of catching these fleeting glimpses, I thought I should mention it to Peg, so I did.

She was interested, and tried to think of a possible identities of the peek-a-boo person or entity, but could not tie it to any specific, known "spirit person."

Almost as a joke she said, "If I didn't know he were still alive, I'd think it might be our friend 'Snoopy'." We both laughed in agreement with that thought and didn't think too much more of it until a day or so later, one of the neighbors came to our door collecting money to buy flowers for the man on the first floor, who had died about a week ago while visiting relatives in the southern part of the country.

Our joke became not so funny when we both realized that our friend "Helpful Henry" had passed away almost exactly the same time I became aware of the peek-a-boo visitor in our apartment. Maybe it was him. Who knows? But it is very interesting to think about.

CHAPTER XXVII
ONE HUNDRED FOLD

As we were preparing to move away from our brick house, we were clearing out what seemed like tons and tons of still useful items, which could no longer be kept for obvious reasons, and which could not readily be sold. These items were hauled, load by load, to a semi-trailer body, parked near Eastwood Mall Shopping Center, which was operated by Goodwill Industries.

The kind gentleman who was the attendant on the truck was named Dick Werner, a man a few years younger than I. He had previously owned several successful businesses, but due to unfortunate circumstances, he lost his businesses and now worked this minimum-wage job for GoodWill Industries.

Dick's wife attended another trailer a few miles away, at another shopping center.

My numerous visits made me a regular and Dick came to know me. The more we talked, the more we shared, and the better became our friendship. Dick and his wife had "found the Lord" and he just loved to give his testimony and tell of how the Lord was taking care of him, even on his minimum-wage salary.

I, in turn, would relate some things to Dick and concur that I also dearly loved God, although, perhaps not precisely in the same manner of worship.

One day, as I stood talking with Dick, something told me to *give him twenty dollars.*

I shrugged it off, but it became insistent. Again and again it told me: *give him twenty dollars.* So I stopped talking in mid-sentence and asked Dick, "Would you be offended if I gave you a twenty-dollar bill? Some little voice keeps telling me to do so."

He looked at me, smiled and slapped my shoulder. "My friend, I would never deprive you of the blessing the Lord will give you for this. Certainly I'll accept your twenty dollars."

About a week later, as I was getting the mail out of our rural mail box at the roadside, I noticed an envelope with very scribbly, scraggly, almost unreadable handwriting. The return address indicated the letter had come from Hilda Wolff in care of some state-operated nursing home or infirmary.

Hilda, as you should recall, is our old widow friend from Lily-Dale, who since has indeed become "infirm" physically, although sharp as a razor mentally.

Hilda had always desired to leave all her worldly possessions to Peg—and I believe her will so stated, but I don't really know that. Two things kept Peg from owning Hilda's house: First you were required to be a member of the Spiritualist Church or the Lily-Dale Assembly in order to own property in the camp, and neither Peg nor I would agree to do that. So we knew that house would never be ours. The other reason was that the State of New York was now impounding Hilda's possessions, as part of the requirement for admission to the home.

I opened the letter and inside was a scribbled check for $800 and a note. "I always wanted to do something for Scott, and now the State has taken everything away from me, but I still have money in the checking account, so please use this check to help pay Scott's college tuition." The next day a second note came from Hilda. "Here is another $1,200.00 for Scott. I have no need for money now, and the State will take it if I don't use it up." —Love Hilda

So now, we had received two thousand greatly needed dollars from such a totally unexpected source. My twenty dollars had come back one hundred times over. I could not wait until my next visit with Dick Werner.

When I jumped out of my car at the Goodwill trailer I was already talking, "Dick, you have got to hear this."

"Just a moment please," he said, as he went to attend a donor who had just driven up. When the lady left, I started again. "Dick, I've got something to tell you."

Dick held up his hand like a stop sign, and said, "It will have to wait. First I've got something to tell you." I agreed to wait. And

Dick proceeded. "You know that twenty dollars you gave me a couple weeks ago?" I said, "Yes. That's what I want to talk about."

Dick continued, "Well, when I got home that night, my son was at home waiting to see me. Maybe you didn't know that my son has had some severe drug problems, and he has been living in a halfway house. He is now "dried out."

"Well he met this nice young woman and they have been attending 'mission' together, and are both now 'living for the Lord.'"

"Anyway, my son came over and told me that the young woman had agreed to go out on a date with him, but he didn't have any money. He wanted twenty dollars, so he could buy each of them a meal, and some gasoline for his car.

"Walt," Dick proceeded, "I looked in my wallet and found your twenty dollar bill. It's all I had, so I gave it to him. Walt, they are going to get married, and my son has since found a pretty good job. If you only knew how I have been praying for that boy, and how thankful I am, that you gave me that twenty dollars."

Well, I now had a few tears to wipe aside, as I told him what my experience had been. He laughed as he said, "I told you I wouldn't deprive you of that blessing."

Sure, it makes a nice story, but I happen to believe in it because God, in his word, says he will bless us abundantly if we follow his path.

CHAPTER XXVIII
THUNDERBIRD

Shortly before my retirement in 1982, I was presented with the opportunity to buy a 1967 Ford Thunderbird (now fifteen years old) in immaculate condition, and with only nineteen thousand miles on it. I could not resist. I bought it as a toy, and kept it safely stored in our attached garage, using only occasionally in the summertime.

Later, with the approaching sale of our home in the works, I was trying to sell my Thunderbird, as I could not wisely keep it while living in an apartment complex.

One day I decided to give the T-Bird a little exercise, so I invited Peg to go out to eat our evening meal and take a ride in the T-Bird. She agreed, on the condition that we go early enough so that she could stop at the bank, which closes at four o'clock. I agreed, and we started out. On the way to the bank, it began to sprinkle rain, and was quite chilly. It was almost four o'clock, so I said to Peg, "I'll pull up to the door behind the cars parked out front and you jump out, so you won't get wet; then I will park the car around the back of the building."

Well, just as Peg opened her door and began to leave the car, the car parked directly in front of my driver's side door began to back out. I yelled out, "Stop. Stop!" while blowing my horn, but to no avail. The young man backed into the side of my beautiful T-Bird with a crunching sound that sickened me. Peg hurried into the bank, as it was now just four o'clock. The young man leaped from his car and began to berate and chastise me for being in his way.

I tired to advise him that he was at fault for not looking to see if the way was clear before he backed out.

We exchanged insurance information and drivers license data, and I insisted on calling the police. The young man said he was leaving and would not wait for the police—and he did leave.

I filed a police report at the security office, inside the mall, since the city police said they would not come out.

After about two months or so of trying to have his insurance pay for the repairs, I finally gave up. His insurance company told me that he had said no such accident had ever occurred. In addition, the accident report which was filed with the security office had disappeared and they said that, as a result, they could only take the position that no such accident had happened. In any event, the value of my Thunderbird had been diminished, as now, even if repaired, it would not be "original" any longer. I finally reconciled myself to selling the "Bird" as is, at a much reduced price, and taking the loss on the chin, which I was able to do.

About the time I was closing the deal to sell the Thunderbird, the young man who backed into me was on my mind. I was both furious, and sympathetic at the same time. When someone is on my mind a lot I usually include that person in my prayers, so, on retiring to bed that night, I spoke to the Lord of the young man. "Lord, I wish you would speak to that young man, and cause him to realize he should tell the truth. I don't want to be the cause of someone living with a lie. Please Lord, wake him up to the fact that you would be much more pleased with him if he told the truth, and cleared his conscience. Amen."

Three days later I received a letter in the mail from his insurance company. The letter said, "We have received a claim form from our client affirming that he backed into your car. Please obtain three estimates and submit them to this office for payment of this claim. Thank You."

Believe it or not, the check from the insurance company added to the price for which I sold the T-Bird totalled exactly what I had paid for the car. *Thank you Lord for the little things too.*

CHAPTER XXIX
WAS IT A MIRACLE?

Earlier in this book I mentioned my rather skeptical attitude regarding mass healing services by evangelists who shout, "Heal! Heal! Heal!" or some similar technique.

My belief in miraculous or "spiritual" healing is profound; it is just the mass-produced variety of healing that I question.

With that out of the way, I can get on with this story.

When our son, Jim, was in his late teens we permitted him to buy a moped, which provided him a means of transportation and a newly found freedom.

One evening, when Jim was not at home, a lady who was a stranger to me, came to our door. When I answered the doorbell she asked me tersely, "Do you have a blonde-haired son who rides a moped?"

"Yes I do," I answered, puzzled by the question.

"Well," she came back sternly, as though admonishing me for having such a son, "He's spread out all over the road, down at the end of the street!"

I thanked her for telling me and immediately dashed to my car in the driveway.

As soon as I turned into the street I could see a traffic jam, and a lot of flashing emergency lights at the outlet of our dead-end street, about a quarter mile down the hill.

I parked as near to the corner as possible and ran over to the intersection, where I saw Jim lying flat on his back in the highway, his moped lying on the berm of the road a few feet away.

As I approached Jim, I told the paramedics that I was Jim's father. They said, "You may speak with him, but don't touch him. He may have a serious back injury."

I watched while they gingerly slid a body board under him. They strapped him to the board and tied his head and neck in a manner that would assure immobility. As they loaded Jim into the ambulance, I dashed home to get Peg, so we could go together to the emergency room. I still did not know exactly what had happened and there did not seem to be any other vehicles involved in the accident.

At the hospital, it seemed like, and it probably was, hours before they would tell us anything.

When the doctor finally approached to talk to us, the news was not good.

The x-rays showed at least one, and possibly two, fractured vertebrae, and Jim was not feeling any sensation in his feet or legs. The doctor tried to reassure us that temporary paralysis is not unusual, and that more x-rays would be taken the next day before they decided on any course of treatment or surgery.

We were advised that the possibility of permanent paralysis did exist and that if the fractures had caused any damage to the spinal cord, the results could be very serious indeed.

Poor Jim was strapped down flat on his back, in traction, and totally immobile. What a way to spend the night, and perhaps much longer.

When we were assured that Jim was as comfortable as possible, Peg and I decided to leave, but not before we said a prayer for Jim's healing.

After we got home we did the usual notifying of family and friends, and with each notification, we asked the entreaty, "Please pray for Jim. He needs all the help he can get." After all were notified, we finally sat down to rest and collect our thoughts. I said to Peg, "Let's pray again and place this all in God's hands. So we held hands and prayed, and believe it or not, we were able to go to bed and get some sleep.

Next morning we got ready and went to the hospital as soon as we would be allowed to see Jim. We anticipated a long bedside vigil while the doctors' decisions would be awaited, and were prepared for the worst.

When we got to Jim's room, he was no longer strapped in bed. He was sitting up; the doctor was at his side.

"How is he?" I questioned the doctor.

"He's just fine. And I don't really understand it, but the x-rays we took today show absolutely no fractures of any kind." He continued, "Jim has already been up walking, and as soon as he is dressed you may take him home with you."

As it turned out Jim had been preparing to make a left turn from the highway onto our street, but he was intimidated by a car that was tailing him but would not pass. So Jim moved to the berm to let the car go past. When he did so, his tires slid on the gravel and he spilled, landing on his back on the pavement.

The car that was bothering him had gone by just as though nothing had happened, and the following cars nearly hit Jim as he lay on the road.

Once again, I offer no explanation of this event. I merely tell you what happened. Whether God intervened and healed Jim's fractures, or whether he never had any to begin with, we will never really know. On the evening of the accident, the doctors had been truly concerned, Jim had been paralyzed in both legs—and the x-rays had shown fractured vertebrae; but after everybody prayed, that all changed. *Thank you, Lord.*

CHAPTER XXX
SPECIAL PEOPLE

Our society has developed a cruel system of eliminating or ignoring those among us who did not quite "fit in," so to speak. I hesitate to enumerate, lest I should leave someone out, but I think you all know what I mean. I refer to that vast collection of lovely folks that we consider "abnormal"—the little people (dwarfs), the fat people, the tall people (freaks), the crippled people, the blind, the deaf, the mentally retarded and those among us who find themselves to be "gay" or homosexual, and even those such as I am with the horrible experience of Tourette's syndrome and all its little embarrassments.

I'm about to tell you a story, which should point out some of the utter hopelessness, fear, and frustration that must consume every ounce of one's being. It involves a young man who is mildly mentally disabled—one who is clever, and smart enough to realize his own limitations, and yet never questions what this is or why it had happened in his life.

I have often wondered just how tough it must be for one such as our Jim, to endure the frustration of knowing that he cannot "measure up" to society's demands.

We can never hope to understand the thought process that controls such a person.

You want the same things in life that everybody else wants, but you know you can never have them—things like a car, a driver's license, a wife, children, a good job, independent living—all those things we take for granted if we are *normal*. Couple that with the frustration of the parents who love the person and who wonder whether he will ever be able to leave home and live on his own or whether he will require confinement in an institution. Perhaps he will become a street vagrant and be victimized by druggies and sexual perverts. Perhaps he will fall into the category of being a "police personality"—one who just can't seem to avoid encounters with the law. The law really makes no provision for folks who "just don't understand" after they have reached adulthood. They no longer fall under the protective cover of being a juvenile.

They are just too much of a bother for most of us to put up with and nobody really knows just how to cope with them, so we try to ignore them.

Don't play with them, don't socialize with them, don't converse with them, and for God's sake, don't work with them, or sit in church with them. They are not socially acceptable.

Are you getting the picture. Are you maybe just a *little* guilty of some of these things yourself? I know I am.

Well try to imagine the feelings and frustrations of a youngster, approaching adulthood, whose loving parents are trying everything possible to "normalize" his lifestyle, and at the same time maybe unburden themselves just a little bit too.

Imagine Jim's feelings and fears in the following story, as his parents are trying to put him out on his own, out of the shelter and protection of Mom and Dad, and into a world which he fears, and in which he feels he cannot cope. What would you do? How would you feel? Please just try to picture yourself in this young man's position as you read what happened.

Then after you read it, try to see the humor in it, along with the tragedy of being a victim of a "not quite normal" mind. Then, when you have a better understanding of Jim's feelings of abandonment and hopelessness, you may learn that we (his parents) learned and maybe then you can, in some small way, make somebody else's life just a little more bearable.

After having tried what we believed to be every conceivable program for rehabilitation or vocational training without success, we decided to try a few "away-from-home" programs, several of which also failed to produce any of the desired results.

Almost as a last resort, we decided to place Jim as a dormitory resident in the Goodwill Industries work training program.

They had excellent training and supervision which we felt certain, would insure proper personal hygiene, diet, dress code, etc. It sounded like the answer to a prayer. We were to arrive at 5:00 P.M.

117

Sunday evening with Jim, so that he could be ready to begin the week's schedule on Monday morning.

About noon on Sunday, upon our arrival home from church services, Jim disappeared with his bicycle. This was not unusual and was no cause for concern, until it got late enough that we would not make our appointment at Goodwill Industries.

Around 5:00 or 6:00 P.M. I decided I had better go looking for Jim. I tried all his usual stopping places and he *had* been there, but hours earlier. I kept looking and at about seven o'clock I saw his bicycle in front of a restaurant. Just as I reached the restaurant door, two police cars were pulling in also. Inside I found Jim and two more police men, who had been interrogating him. The restaurant manager had become alarmed because Jim had been sitting at the counter for hours, in a "daze", and in his concern, he had called the police.

I identified myself as Jim's father and one police officer, a state patrolman, began to relate his findings.

Jim had told him that two hoodlums had taken him out into a nearby wooded field and forced him to drink whiskey and get drunk. The patrolman very wisely asked me if Jim had ever fantasized. I answered, "Yes. Frequently. He also suffers *petit mal* seizures, which put him into a trance-like state when he is under extreme stress."

"Well," said the officer, "I thought so because he has no sign of alcohol on his breath and he's been sitting in this place for hours and hours. He could not have been abducted as he said."

Everyone was relieved that I appeared and explained the situation and I was permitted to take Jim home. Jim had successfully avoided his dreaded appointment at Goodwill Industries.

The next morning I was at work and still stewing about what to do, when my office phone rang. It was Peg. Scott was now rebelling at going to school (he had become a school-a-phobic) and refused to get out of bed. I had previously told Peg to call me, and even if it would cost me my job, I would come home, get Scott up, and physically deliver him to school. So I said to Peg, "Okay. Since I must come home anyway, go ahead and get Jim up and get ready to take him to Goodwill. After I deliver Scott to school, we'll take Jim to Youngstown as arranged, only one day late.

All went as planned. Scott was reluctantly delivered to Howland High School (it was gym day) and we now took Jim to the Goodwill workshop.

We were cordially greeted and assured that the one-day delay would work no hardship. We all toured the facility, saw what was to be Jim's room, met his roommate, and everything seemed fine—to Peg and me. Jim gave no overt indication of serious discomfort and seemed to be resolved to the situation. We prepared to leave, so he could get on with his schedule.

The very nice young woman, who was our tour guide, happened to be someone we had met previously at mental health group meetings, and was a high official of the Epilepsy Foundation.

I took her aside and quietly whispered to her so Jim could not hear, "Please watch him very closely. He is traumatized and will need close supervision for a few days." I then asked her, "What do your people do about lunch?"

She responded, "Oh, they get an hour off and can do whatever they want. They can even go out to eat if they so choose."

When I heard that I said to her, "Well, please don't let Jim go out today. Don't let him out of your sight until he calms down." She nodded, smiled knowingly and assured me that I had nothing to worry about. Jim would be "taken care of."

With that assurance, Peg and I left to make the fifteen-mile trip home for our own lunch. On the way I said to Peg, "Listen. Why don't you prepare us some lunch, and while you do that, I'll run down to the high school and speak to Scott's counselor about his situation!" Peg agreed, and after dropping her off at home, I went to the school, about two miles or less from home. When I arrived at the school office, the secretary (who was a long-time acquaintance of ours) said to me, "Walt. You are to call Peg. I think something's wrong with Scott."

How could that be? I thought to myself. *He's right here in school. I brought him myself.*

I called Peg. The message had been misunderstood. Scott was fine, but Jim—that was something else.

"What's wrong?" I asked. "We just dropped him off at Goodwill an hour ago!"

She said, "I don't know. I don't understand it, but the Youngstown Police Department called and they have Jim in jail for bank robbery."

"What? What did you say? Bank robbery?" I began to laugh. "That is impossible. It must be a mistake. I'll be right there and we'll go down there and find out what's going on. You had better call Goodwill and see if Jim is okay there."

When I arrived at home, Peg verified that Jim was indeed in jail.

The nice lady who had not heeded my warnings and had let Jim go out for lunch, said that the last she saw him was when the police took him away in a patrol car.

When we arrived at the police station, we met with a sergeant of detectives, who would not give us any information. He said, "Bank robbery is a federal offense and we must wait until the FBI gets here. They are on the way."

After about an hour, two agents came in and were shortly directed to us. They asked us, "What happened here?" I looked startled and answered, "What do you mean, *what happened here?* We dropped our son off at Goodwill Industries several hours ago and now he's in jail and nobody will tell us why."

The agent appeared shocked that we did not yet know what had happened, so they explained it to us this way.

Jim had entered the bank (which is in a shopping center across the street from Goodwill Industries), approached a teller's cage, pointed a knife at the teller and told her, "This is a holdup." Of course, the alarm was sounded and it just so happened there was a patrol car about two hundred feet from the bank. Jim ran out of the bank empty handed, save for the paring knife, which he threw on the pavement as he ran towards the Goodwill Industries building.

Several back-up police cars were, by that time, arriving, and with guns drawn, they were all commanding Jim to stop. But Jim kept on running, and thank God, no shots were fired. Several (they said six) police officers had caught him and manhandled him to the Goodwill parking lot pavement, where he was rapped with billy clubs, subdued, handcuffed, and taken to jail.

After all this explanation, Peg and I were totally dumbfounded and I said to the FBI agents, "I need time to think. I can't believe this."

The agents were especially kind and understanding and one of them said to me, "You know, you look familiar to me. I've met you somewhere before. Are you active in church work?" he asked. "Yes, I am—or have been quite a bit." "That must be it, he said, "because I'm sure that I know you."

Then the other agent spoke up. "Does Jim fantasize?" he asked.

Now this was strange—this was the exact same question the policeman had asked me yesterday in Warren. "Why would you ask that?" I responded.

"Well," the agent continued, "I have a brother who is mentally disabled and that gives me some understanding of what we may be up against here." He went on to explain, "Jim told us that two black men in a red Camaro drove into the plaza and called him over to their car. He said the one on the passenger side pointed a gun at him, and give him the knife and a paper bag and said to him, 'Take this and go in and rob that bank or I'll kill you, I'll be standing outside by the door, watching and if you don't do it I'll kill you.'" The agent went on, "Jim is very insistent about this and he is very convincing. But we have no evidence to support his story."

Then he asked me directly, "Do you think he could be fantasizing?"

"I don't know," I answered. "That's quite a detailed story for him to invent."

The agent then told us something that brought chills to our spines. They said, "You know, today is the first day of the new mayor's term in office and he has appointed a new chief of police, who is also starting his first day today. And since crime had been a major issue in the campaign, the successful capture of a bank robber on the spot would be a big publicity 'plus.' So they may decide to ride this for all it's worth."

We were then advised to go home, and to return at 9:00 A.M. the next morning.

I have no idea what transpired next, but when we returned the next morning, the agents were waiting for us. They had found out that Jim purchased the paring knife in a variety store in the plaza, and that the story of the two black men in a red car had indeed been a fantasy. They had checked out my story of the "Goodwill" episode, and had made up their minds.

"Mr. Cameron," the agent began, "we have no reason to believe a crime was committed. We don't care to detain Jim. As far as we are concerned you can take Jim home with you, but you will have to wait to see if the chief of police wants to do anything with it on a local basis."

The two FBI angels—excuse me—I mean agents, waited with us, and when the word came down that the chief had decided not to press the matter either, they smiled, shook our hands and said "God bless you folks and good luck to you in the future."

Jim was now delivered to us and given a stern lecture by the lieutenant, before being allowed to go home with us.

You tell me that God had not sent his own guardian angels to look after that situation and I'll call you insensitive and totally unbelieving.

Now, we were back to square one. Jim was back home again, and the problem of what to do about Jim was still staring us in the face. But we had learned something; we were now aware of the sheer terror Jim must have had over "being shoved out" of his comfortable, secure lifestyle.

We soon heard about a group boarding home, also on the North Side of Youngstown. There they would provide a comfortable home with good, nourishing meals and the loving attention of a motherly black lady named Dorothy. To our great surprise, Jim immediately took a liking to Dorothy and decided he would like to try living in her house. (She did not own it: she was the cook and manager.)

Jim learned to know some new people, began some new friendships, and just loved Dorothy and her very special scalloped potatoes, which he insisted his mother must learn to make.

We, as well as Jim, soon learned that there existed a network of people in the North Side of Youngstown who were all consumers of the Ohio Department of Mental Health Services. Much to the concern and consternation of the North Side Citizen's Coalition, they lived in group homes, boarding homes, even private homes and apartments, which they rented on a "shared" basis.

In essence, these wonderful, handicapped people had massed together to form their own little subculture. The North Side residents didn't like it. Many of the consumers were showing up at church services, where coffee and donuts or lunches were served after church was over; neither the clergy nor the faithful knew what to do about it.

Jim soon took up with a small group of his peers and they rented a row house together. Jim got a newspaper route, and did quite well along with his SSI check.

He maintained his association in the clannish subculture and got involved when someone of them needed a helping hand, but he preferred living alone, so we did not object.

We would visit him on Saturdays or Sundays, and make a grocery and/or clothing shopping excursion to the shopping center a few miles away, take in a restaurant meal and an ice cream treat and call it a day. Jim seemed to flourish in this lifestyle and did quite well at meeting his bills, feeding himself and keeping his place clean and liveable.

My whole point here is that the mental health professionals, who are so taken up with de-institutionalizing mental health patients, should take notice of what these folks really want, and then see if we can't somehow come up with a way to provide it.

They simply want to live a life as "normally" as possible, within the confines of their own abilities, and to be left alone.

Some of them can "make it" in an apartment, or private home with a minimum of counsel from a case worker. Others would do better in a group-home setting. Still others would require a more structured dormitory-like setting, with proper supervision and enough freedom and privacy to lead a near-normal existence, and yet still be in close touch with their friends and peers, with whom they seem most comfortable.

God only knows why the professionals refuse to recognize this simple, common denominator of understanding.

They seem only to know how to build bigger and fancier mental health centers and to staff them with well-meaning desk sitters, who need bigger salaries and more benefits, so that soon the mental health service monster we have created is more interested in self preservation and growth, than it is in getting the dollars and the services to those poor folks who really need it.

Fortunately our own situation is better than we could ever have hoped it would be. We moved Jim to Arizona where he can still be near enough to feel the security blanket of Mom and Dad, but far enough that he knows he must make it on his own.

His Gramma Grace always said her little angel would make an excellent grocer and she was right. Jim is as happy in his lifestyle as anyone could be. He lives in a small mobile home park and enjoys every moment that he's on duty at a nearby supermarket.

If every person on earth could achieve as much, according to their individual abilities, as Jim has, this would be a wonderful world indeed.

CHAPTER XXXI WAS IT REAL?

I will leave you with "something to think about." Whatever you infer from this, I want it to be your own, not something planted by me. You can decide if I have been blessed—or cursed. If I have done with my life, a good thing—or if I have missed the most important message of all by not following the answer to my own challenge. If so, has this book somehow made amends—or am I just an over imaginative, dreamy-eyed fool? In either case, it has been a very interesting and challenging walk down life's pathway, and I am at peace with God.

When I cross over there I will have passed, or failed—as will you, and you, and you, and you.

Now, you decide. It was a beautiful, warm August evening while I was living at my sister's home and just about to start the fall term at Newton Falls High School. I was home alone, seated at the kitchen table, reading the bible I had just purchased, which I intended to present to "my girl"—the girl I thought was *the one*—until Peg stole my heart away.

I decided to "throw out a fleece" to God, and prayed, "Lord, do you want me in the ministry or in any full-time Christian work? If you do, then, show me a cross in the sky. When I look at the sky, show me a vivid, genuine, geometric cross, and I will know what your answer is. Amen!"

I raised my head, looked out through the open kitchen door, through the screen door, and immediately I saw a perfect, bright golden cross. I almost fell off the chair. I looked again, I squinted, I peered—the cross was vivid. I now began to realize that at the center of the cross was a bright yellow, rising full moon.

I walked over to the screen door and looked closer. The cross was brilliant. I wanted a better look so I stepped outside. The cross disappeared, but the full moon shone brightly. I went back into the kitchen and the cross returned, back outside and the cross disappeared. Suddenly, with great disappointment, I realized that the screen wire in the door was refracting the moon's light and creating what appeared to be a cross. It wasn't really there and all my excitement faded away. I now felt foolish and decided I was being a little silly to have thought that really could have happened. You know the feeling: It's the same way you feel when that figure you thought you saw standing in the dark turns out to be a lamp that someone hung a sweater over—or was it? Had I been given what I asked for, then expected too much?

I was very young then, but I have had recurring thoughts, throughout my life, about that moment and that decision.

So please, watch and listen and heed that "still, small voice" and when you ask for something "in His name, it will be given unto you." Pay close attention, so as not to miss it after you ask.

And as for my question, *Have I been blessed or cursed?* Well, I will answer it for you. Yes, I have truly been blessed. I have known the pain of disappointment, the anxiety of frustration, the cuts and bruises of the rocky climb up the numerous mountains that have been placed in my pathway.

Together my devoted wife and I have climbed our mountains and followed our rainbows and realized our dreams.

As Dr. Martin Luther King once said, "I have been to the mountain top, and I have a dream." Dr. King did not live to see his dream come true. I have been much more fortunate. I have lived to see some of mine come true.

Against seemingly impossible odds, both of my sons have overcome many obstacles and have succeeded in their desire to be productive citizens. No miracle God ever performed could surpass the peace and satisfaction that our children have provided for Peg and me. The following birthday greeting I received from Jim says it all:

May 11, 1991

To the BEST DAD in the WORLD.
He's always there when you need him
And I know you're the best

125

May this be your day
And better days ahead
FOR THE BEST
Many best wishes, for today
And always
HAPPY BIRTHDAY,
Your son, JAMES.

There is no mountain high enough to top the feeling I had when I read that handwritten greeting, from a son of whom I am so proud.

If I leave no other legacy to this earth but my three children, and their children, I will have been successful in my mission in this life.

THE END

POSTSCRIPT

Since the completion of the manuscript of this book, I have had the gnawing feeling that it really does not provide the reader with a proper conclusion. I had written a final chapter which I deleted at the suggestion of several people., Many things have occurred since the publishing process began that have caused me to include this Postscript chapter. I have also included a substantial portion of that which was to have been the final chapter, so now I feel better about the whole book.

"ergo"

I have always been a strong proponent of "Substantive evidence." The things of which I have written about the occurrences in my life are absolute proof to me that there truly is a dimension of super intelligence which reaches beyond the physical.

I realize that these things cannot be proven to you; you have only my word that they did happen. Yet you must also understand that I cannot disbelieve, because I was there—it happened to me. I don't need to question the truth of it.

I know!

It is only logical then to deduce from such evidence that there is life after physical death, and that indicates the existence of a greater power, a higher form of life that is in control of all life.

This deduction—or, more correctly, this verification of what I had already believed—has set my faith forever. So many biblical truths exist which cannot be refuted that it boggles my mind to hear of people who profess to be atheistic.

In the Christian bible, God challenges us to put Him to the test; not to prove his existence, but rather to prove the reality of his promise, to those who will believe. He proves it from the twenty-third Psalm, which everyone knows, to the promise of Jesus, in St. John Chapter 14, verses thirteen and fourteen.

13: And whatsoever ye shall ask in my name, that I will do, that the Father may be glorified in the Son.

14: If ye shall ask *anything* in my name, *I will* do it.

What I have learned from all these unique experiences, I'm not sure. God's mystery is his own. He will reveal himself in his own way and in his own chosen time. But I believe this: there are Angels, there are Spirits, and there is no death. There is only physical death for all of us, and eternal torment for the unbelievers, or rather for the evil ones.

I cannot presume to believe that whoever or whatever it is that comes to me unsolicited and gives me insight into unusual matters could be evil or demonic. I do believe it could be a "Guardian Angel," or even a manifestation of God's own Holy Spirit. After all, when you place your life in His hands, you should not be surprised when He looks after your affairs.

I really did not intend to sermonize, but I felt it important to state my position on these matters.

As a final closing story, I will relate two occurrences that have happened since the first thirty chapters were sent to the publishing house.

My daughter has always been my special "Squirt." (a nickname I pinned on her early in her life). She is one of the brightest lights in my life. She is a devout "Charismatic Christian," adamant in her objections to things related to Metaphysics or Spirit manifestations. She sees those as a segment of the Occult, and as such, evil. She openly does not agree with the publishing of this book since, in her mind it will tend to lead people astray of God. She does not dispute the truth of the events; rather, she attests to many of them. She says, "I know they are true, I lived with it all my life. As a child I never knew what to expect next, never knew who would be walking the halls in our home. It's just that I don't like it and I don't wish to have my children exposed to it." I guess the fundamental difference is that her mother and I are certain that we will be together with her in the other side of life or Heaven, whereas Diane knows she will be there but she as serious misgivings as to whether Mom and Dad will make it.

128

Anyway, the two events, which I found interesting enough to prompt me to add this Postscript chapter, are as follows.

Peg and I were visiting Diane and her family in Ohio last summer. I allowed them to read my manuscript. Laura and Patricia, however, were not permitted by their mother to read it. Doug, being a little older, has his own personal computer, so he took the disk and read it from his computer monitor without permission.

The morning after Diane had finished reading it, we were about to have coffee, and I was looking for a small paper plate to hold my luscious-looking doughnut. I had looked through he kitchen cabinets, and had just opened the doors of the last cabinet when Diane stepped up behind me to ask what it was that I was looking for. The cabinet was a wall cabinet, mounted above the countertop, and as such was rather high. When I opened the double doors on the cabinet, I could see large paper plates on the lower shelf but no small ones. I could not see what was on the top shelf as it was too high for my vision. As Diane approached me from behind, and before she could speak, I asked, "Don't you have any small paper plates?" I was not touching the cabinet or its doors at this time, but the moment I uttered my question, something came flying out of the top shelf of the cabinet. Instead of falling to the countertop below or to the floor, the flying object did a somersault in mid-air, reversed direction, and landed smack dab dead center on top of the pile of large paper plates on the lower shelf of the cabinet. As it landed I could see it was a stack of about a dozen or so small paper plates. Diane made an exclamation something like, "Whoo my goodness." I turned to look at her and just smiled, saying nothing. Several days later, when I brought up the subject of the plates to Diane, she had this to say: "You don't think that was something spooky do you? I certainly don't. You must have bumped the cupboard or something to cause those plates to fall out."

I answered, "Yes, and I suppose I caused them to turn around and fly back into the cabinet instead of falling to the floor as they should have? Don't you find it interesting that small paper plates are exactly what I was looking for, and that they just happened to land on the large paper plates, exactly where I had been looking?"

She replied, "Oh, I don't know about that," and the conversation ended. Perhaps she is right about it, but I'll bet it would shake up old Isaac Newton if he had seen it.

The other event involves my concern over my ability to cover the expense of publishing this book. I guess in today's society the cost isn't all that great, but it was enough that I felt it necessary to go the paperback route and eliminate the numerous photos I had originally planned to use. I opted to go with this very capable subsidy publisher rather than risk the lottery of the large publishing houses. I wanted this book published, so I dared not risk rejection. Anyway every time I would begin to worry about how to cover the cost of publishing, my non-voice voice would speak to me saying, "The funds will be provided." As time passed by, and no funds were "being provided," I began to worry again. Once more my "Something" told me, "I told you the funds will be provided, now stop your worrying." I told Peg about what had occurred and that "I guess I had better stop worrying."

She said, "Of course you should stop it, that's what I've been telling you all along." It took at least eight or ten times for the non-voice to tell me before I began to believe it, but once I decided to really believe it, something strange and wonderful happened. I noticed in the daily stock reports in the newspaper that one of our few remaining, and near dormant holdings, was moving up. I phoned my investment broker to inquire as to the reason. I was informed that the company had just settled a long standing negotiation with the I.R.S., and that the excess from the funds allocated to the worst case scenario of the tax negotiations would be distributed to the share holders. In about two months I would be receiving a check for an amount sufficient to cover the cost of the publishing. "Praise the Lord," He has kept His promise as always. It is only our lack of faith that holds Him back from fulfilling His promise.

Diane has told me that she is praying that "God's will might be done" concerning the fortunes of this book. I told her that I am doing the same thing. I guess we sort of really hope the same thing. My prayer is that I may have convinced some non-believers to turn to God as the result of reading this book. I kind of believe that she is praying the same thing. And now I am finished, and I feel much better about our book. God Bless you and have faith.